PUBLIC SPEAKING

Effective Communication With Amazing Self Confidence to Master Social Skills and Presentation

(Kick Stage Fear, Boost Your Charisma to Make a Great Speech and Win Over Any Audience)

Nancy Davies

Published by Rob Miles

© **Nancy Davies**

All Rights Reserved

Public Speaking: Effective Communication With Amazing Self Confidence to Master Social Skills and Presentation (Kick Stage Fear, Boost Your Charisma to Make a Great Speech and Win Over Any Audience)

ISBN 978-1-989990-05-6

All rights reserved. No part of this guide may be reproduced in any form without permission in writing from the publisher except in the case of brief quotations embodied in critical articles or reviews.

Legal & Disclaimer

The information contained in this book is not designed to replace or take the place of any form of medicine or professional medical advice. The information in this book has been provided for educational and entertainment purposes only.

The information contained in this book has been compiled from sources deemed reliable, and it is accurate to the best of the Author's knowledge; however, the Author cannot guarantee its accuracy and validity and cannot be held liable for any errors or omissions. Changes are periodically made to this book. You must consult your doctor or get professional medical advice before using any of the suggested remedies, techniques, or information in this book.

Upon using the information contained in this book, you agree to hold harmless the Author from and against any damages, costs, and expenses, including any legal fees potentially resulting from the application of any of the information provided by this guide. This disclaimer applies to any damages or injury caused by the use and application, whether directly or indirectly, of any advice or information presented, whether for breach of contract, tort, negligence, personal injury, criminal intent, or under any other cause of action.

You agree to accept all risks of using the information presented inside this book. You need to consult a professional medical practitioner in order to ensure you are both able and healthy enough to participate in this program.

Table of Contents

INTRODUCTION 1

CHAPTER 1: ETHOS, PATHOS, LOGOS 4

CHAPTER 2: UNDERSTANDING THE ROOT CAUSE OF PUBLIC SPEAKING ANXIETY 8

CHAPTER 3: USING SPEECHES AND PRESENTATIONS 17

CHAPTER 4: 10 STEPS TO MASTER THE ART OF PUBLIC SPEAKING 22

CHAPTER 5: GETTING TO KNOW YOURSELF 31

CHAPTER 6: PRACTISE, REHEARSE AND VISUALIZE 37

CHAPTER 7: BUILD YOUR CONFIDENCE 48

CHAPTER 8: YOUR SIGNATURE LOOK 58

CHAPTER 9: WHERE DO I BEGIN WHEN CRAFTING MESSAGES THAT MATTER? 70

CHAPTER 10: ASSESSMENT 79

CHAPTER 11: STEPS OF HOW TO CONTROL YOURSELF 82

CHAPTER 12: ON GETTING A LOVE LIFE 91

CHAPTER 13: ORGANIZING AND OUTLINING 95

CHAPTER 14: THE TYPES OF SPEECH 102

CHAPTER 15: I'VE GOT THE DORMANT RUNNER BLUES. 108

CHAPTER 16: COPING WITH THE UNEXPECTED 115

CHAPTER 17: DON'T ALLOW STAGE FRIGHT STOP YOU FROM MAKING A POWERFUL SPEECH 119

CHAPTER 18: PROVEN WAYS TO GRAB THE AUDIENCES' ATTENTION 124

CHAPTER 19: COMMUNICATION IN MARRIAGE 134

CHAPTER 20: THE GRAND FINALE. INCITING ACTION IN YOUR FINAL MINUTES 151

CHAPTER 21: THE HEART OF THE MATTER: 156

CHAPTER 22: USE VISUAL AIDS, ILLUSTRATIONS 192

CONCLUSION 197

Introduction

Besides a visit to the dentist, nothing else strikes more fear into people's hearts than the thought of speaking before an audience. Jerry Seinfeld, a famous American comedian and actor, took it a step further when he claimed that people are generally more afraid of public speaking than they are of death.

While this might be an exaggeration, studies have shown that he is not too far off. Social scientists claim that our fear of standing before an audience is deeply ingrained in the most primitive part of our brains. According to this theory, survival depends on being part of the crowd, of going with the flow instead of standing out and being the center of attention.

Psychologists have even come up with a term for this: glossophobia. In simple English, we would call it "speech anxiety," from the Greek glosso for tongue and phobia for extreme fear. Do note, however, that there are many who would erroneously use that term to also describe stage fright, which is topophobia.

Another theory states that our fear of public speaking stems from a fear of rejection and of being eaten by predators. No, seriously. According to Glenn Croston, a biologist, researcher, and author, rejection in early human societies was akin to death. For humans to survive in a hostile world, acceptance in a group was essential. To be rejected was to be alone, and to be alone was to face the threat of predators on one's own, thus reducing the chances of survival.

So maybe Seinfeld wasn't too far off, huh?

Fortunately, we have come a long way since those days. If you do find yourself in a position where you have to give a speech or a public presentation, relax. In fact, that's actually the first key to being a successful public speaker, by the way: the ability to relax.

While rejection is a very real possibility (I said relax!), there are very few fanged predators left out there to be afraid of... at least according to National Geographic.

Miraculously, it seems that there are certain people out there who were simply born to be natural public speakers. Chances are, however, that you are not one of them. Otherwise, you wouldn't be reading this, now would you? But there is a secret to those so-called "natural" public speakers — people who seem so comfortable addressing large crowds as if they were put here on earth to do just that.

What's their secret?

Their secret is that most, if not all of them, were taught how to properly speak to an audience. That's right. It's a skill that can be taught. That's good news for you, because it means that you, too, can be taught.

Chapter 1: Ethos, Pathos, Logos

Aristotle's Guide to Rhetoric

The ancient Greek philosopher Aristotle wrote a masterful guide to persuasive public speaking called Rhetoric. Aristotle's work is regarded by most rhetoricians as "the most important single work on persuasion ever written." It has also been said that "all subsequent rhetorical theory is but a series of responses to issues raised" by Aristotle's Rhetoric.

In Rhetoric, Aristotle outlines three different methods of persuasion:

Ethos. Ethos refers to attempting to persuade people by appealing to one's credibility. For example, a doctor rarely has any trouble "persuading" his or her patients to take a certain medication or course of action. You can apply this to your own speeches by referring to sources of credibility. For example, have you successfully done something like this before? Do you have a degree on this topic? Are you an industry expert? A professor or executive with inside knowledge on this particular topic?

Pathos. Pathos refers to appealing to the audience's emotions, such as by pointing out an injustice, eliciting sympathy, agreeing with values shared by the audience, etc. Pathos can also include appeals to hope (e.g. Obama's "Hope" slogan and speeches) or painting a picture of a positive future resulting from following the proposed cause of action (e.g. Martin Luther King's "I Have a Dream" speech). Pathos also includes appeals to fear and other negative emotions, for example Donald Trump frequently appealed to fear during his 2016 presidential campaign. Here is a definition of "pathos" in Aristotle's words: "Secondly, persuasion may come through the hearers, when the speech stirs their emotions."

Logos. Logos refers to logic. For example, the statement, "All men are mortal,

Socrates is a man, therefore Socrates is mortal," is rather convincing due to it's appeal to logic. Logos also includes referring to facts, figures, and other forms of evidence that back up your argument.

The use of ethos, pathos, and logos as rhetorical devices can be summarised as follows: before you can persuade an audience, they must first accept you as credible (ethos); your audience must then feel an emotional connection with you and/or your message, because people predominantly think and act based on emotion (pathos); finally, your argument should make sense and be backed up with facts and figures and other evidence.

Credibility. Feeling. Logic.

They must feel that you're an expert or a trustworthy source. They must feel some sort of emotion that tugs them in the direction you want (love, sympathy, hate, envy, fear, hope, etc.). And they must feel that your argument is based on logic and facts.

You may have noticed that I repeatedly used the word "feel." This is not a mistake. Everything comes down to the way your audience feels. Feeling, feeling, feeling.

Dodgy salesmen can make a quick buck by purporting themselves as a credible source, appealing to the buyers emotion (e.g. fear or hope), and making up (or exaggerating or misusing) facts. They can be slick and charming, making their victim feel as if they can trust them.

Lesson: When seeking to persuade an audience through your speech, make sure to incorporate references to your credibility, an emotional component, as well as references to facts, figures, and evidence.

Chapter 2: Understanding The Root Cause Of Public Speaking Anxiety

Ironically, people fear public speaking more than they fear death. There are studies that show death ranking only second to the main source of fear for most people. It's actually why you often hear people remark "He's dying up there" if a speaker looks overly anxious or nervous. This may sound unbelievable, but it is sadly true. So your anxiety is actually more common than you imagined. But one great thing about it being so common is that there have been numerous techniques and strategies developed to overcome it.

Before you start tackling this fear that you may at times think is unfounded and debilitating, you first need to understand what its root cause is. Below are some of the common reasons why public speaking has become one of the most dreaded experiences for many:

Its reputation precedes itself

Urban legends and ghost stories get a lot of hype and become extra frightening because of the numerous details that different people add to the original story. What once was a run of the mill ghost story turns into a terrifying tale. This is because people add elements that they are personally afraid of. For example, a story about a woman dressed in white who hitchhikes and vanishes while inside the car can become more chilling with more gory details.

When a person who is afraid of blood can retell the story and embellish it a little bit. The woman's clothes are no longer just white but are now bloodstained as well. Her face is also bloody and when she vanishes, she leaves a pool of blood where she once sat. Somebody who hears this story can add some more details when he or she retells the story. And as more people tell the story, the more frightening it becomes.

Public speaking goes through the same metamorphosis. As more and more people share their own humiliating and nail biting public speaking experiences, the scarier it becomes to other people. Most of the reasons you have for being afraid of standing up and talking in front of an audience may be based on what happened to your friends or people you know.

You may have attended a wedding where the maid of honor or best man made the most embarrassing and inappropriate toast. You sat and cringed along with everybody else. You thanked your lucky stars that it had not been you in their shoes. You may have also comforted a friend who fell over while making a sales presentation to a very important client.

Even if you have never experienced being booed at or forgetting what you were going to say, hearing about other people's bad experiences turn these from something that's remotely possible to something that is highly likely to happen to you. So where you were simply just shy before, you end up getting absolutely terrified of public speaking. Your cause of anxiety has become bigger as you add your own fears with that of others.

Hearing stories or witnessing Murphy's Law in action has made you afraid of stepping into the spotlight. This may be one of the reasons why you feel overly anxious about public speaking.

Fear of Rejection

Your sense of self preservation protects you from things that may cause you physical, mental and emotional harm. These include activities that may be dangerous such as jumping off a cliff or crossing the street with cars zipping by. These also include actions where you feel uncomfortable or humiliated. Standing in front of a crowd opens you to scrutiny which may have embarrassing results.

You get stressed with the fear that other people may not accept what you are saying, how you are saying it, and even how you look while stating your point. You think about people standing up and walking out because they do not agree with what you are saying. You are afraid of cracking a joke and finding out that nobody else but you found it funny.

By placing yourself at the center of attention, you expose yourself to rejection. This can be a scary experience as you go against human nature which is to stay within the limits of what you find comfortable and reassuring. As a result, you can start feeling physical symptoms such as nausea, cold sweats, and dizziness. When this happens, you find yourself unable to fully function. So, despite knowing what you want to say, you have difficulty finding the right words. There are even times when you are unable to literally open your mouth to utter anything intelligible.

Since these are not instances where you would find yourself proud, you tend to avoid putting yourself in situations that have these results. Your body automatically goes into a fight or flight mode with the latter obviously winning. Your fear of being rejected by the people listening turn public speaking into an event that you would do your best to avoid at all cost.

Taking It Personal

While your personality has a lot to do with the success of your speech or presentation, it is not the end all and be all of public speaking. There are different elements that also influence how the audience will behave. Among these elements are relevant content and delivery. Unfortunately, getting a negative reaction often discourages individuals who are still in the process of learning to deliver an effective speech. Hearing comments or getting interrupted feels personal so you cannot help but feel as though you are being attacked.

You increase the stress level by worrying about how your audience perceives you as a person and not as a speaker. You dread having to stand in front and be the object of scrutiny. You wonder whether your listeners agree with you or think you are merely babbling about sheer nonsense. With so much stress involved in agonizing over everybody's opinion of you, you start getting more anxious about the actual speaking experience.

The X-Factor

Some people are born with it and some are not. This is what most talent competitions would want the entire world to believe. You are either born with the ability to excel in a certain skill or you were meant for something else. Much as it sounds like a universal truth, it is merely a cop out that most people choose to hide behind. You have most probably heard people say that they simply were not meant to do something. You may have perhaps even uttered those words yourself in a moment of weakness.

But if that statement was actually true, then there would not be any need for school or any type of training and education. While certain people are indeed naturals, a skill is something that can be developed and improved. Believing that one has to be born with the innate talent can certainly increase the stress level involved in public speaking. Believing this can actually result in you being even more reluctant to immerse yourself in the experience of being in front and making a speech or presentation.

Public speaking is a skill that can be developed. It is like how babies learn how to walk. They do not come out of the womb walking. It is something that they need to learn through stages. They first learn to roll over and then crawl. And before they even get walking, they fall over and get bruised along the process. It is the same for public speaking. It is not something that you become good at overnight, but it is certainly something you can excel at with enough practice and effort.

Once Bitten, Twice Shy

Having a previous bad experience can also put you off and make you dread public speaking. You may have had equipment malfunction or had hecklers while addressing an audience in the past that has caused you to be wary of being put in the same situation. It is almost the same as avoiding driving through a big pothole on the street where you always pass by. You know it is there and you know it may cause you some damage so you take extra precautions against it. Your mind remembers the stress you went through during the previous incident so it sends up alarm bells. This is why it becomes extra challenging for you to repeat the experience as you are nervous about going through the same challenges

Whatever your reason is for being afraid of standing in front of an audience to speak, it is possible to overcome this fear. The key is proper preparation and a lot of practice.

Chapter 3: Using Speeches And Presentations

A late study, promoting officials were asked what they considered the comprehensive most imperative business resource for an innovative expert to have other than ability. The greater part of respondents, 55 percent to be precise, said solid presentation skills. Particular industry experience positioned a removed second with 23 percent; just 3 percent referred to administration experience. The review was directed by an independent research firm and included reactions from 200 promoting officials among the main 1,000 U.S. promoting offices.

MBA graduates thought the capacity to discuss viable with someone else was the absolute most valuable ability in their vocation. "Capacity to convey adequately is the most critical ability you can have," says Daybreak Rosenberg McKay, profession arranging guide at About.com, Inc.

We as a whole need to pitch our thoughts and positions. The main issue is that your belief might be justified regardless of a fortune, yet if you can't convey it unmistakably and with the fitting effect your message may get lost or not persuade a crowd of people. Your incredible thought may get to be useless.

Relational abilities are critical and open talking is an obvious need to anybody seeking to an authority position. I have met exceptionally smart individuals that can't adequately impart even essential data to people around them. They are not influential pioneers and are not as fruitful as they could be. Genuinely extraordinary officials and useful group business pioneers are extremely agreeable communicators. They utilize straightforward dialect that the panel of onlookers can identify with. Truth be told I find that the best communicators are ones that utilization the crowd's dialect and expressions. This exclusive bodes well yet is so frequently missed.

1. Consider your gathering of people deliberately. What dialect or language ought to be maintained a strategic distance from? If language is essential (and unequivocally address this), then characterize any irregular or extraordinary terms (maybe more that once).

2. Have a readied presentation for the individual that will present you. The performance ought to express your name, set up validity with a bio that has a fortifying illustration or two and gives the title of the discourse.

3. In your opening let the gathering of people know to what extent the presentation or discussion will last. Fill them in regarding whether there will be an inquiry and answer session toward the end or whether you will be accessible to answer addresses later. Clarify when and where you will be.

4. If you are going to make a presentation with a slide indicate then utilize this to keep yourself on track yet, don't read your slides and dependable face and look at the group of onlookers. At the point when looking don't key a lot on a particular individual and convey your eye contact about the room.

5. Never apologize for being anxious. It just makes the gathering of people apprehensive and numerous in the group of onlookers would not have taken note.

6. Use connecting with dialect, for example, "Envision if . . ." or "Have you ever considered . . ." or recount a story that catches the consideration of the gathering of people as an opening. I have heard some at Toastmasters allude to these expressions as mesmerizing stems. They don't entrance yet they get the crowd in the inclination or get the gathering of people to feel the tone of the discourse or presentation better.

7. Utilize your voice to accentuate watchwords or expressions. Try not to be monotone - talk with energy.

8. Use non-verbal communication to stress watchwords or key focuses. Rehearse your discourse or presentation ahead of time to calibrate your non-verbal communication and your movements.

9. Give a synopsis and a solid conclusion. Your outline and conclusion ought to accentuate the real purposes of the presentation or discourse.

10. Try not to leave the podium unattended when wrapped up. Continuously disregard control to the individual running the meeting or the gathering or to the Speaker. The platform should never be left unattended.

Conveying a discourse or having a high-effect presentation is a fundamental expertise in today's dynamic commercial center. With arranging and some practice you can turn out to be great it. Search for chances to talk and present as one of the key things to overcome is an apprehension of speaking. By talking and introducing more your will turn out to be more alright with it.

Chapter 4: 10 Steps To Master The Art Of Public Speaking

Public speaking is an art, centered around delivering a speech or a presentation in front of an audience. Public speaking in front of a group takes a lot of courage and preparation. You need to develop the appropriate skills in order to be an effective public speaker. Let's examine the ten key characteristics that excellent public speakers portray.

Knowledge

It is important that you know exactly what you are talking about. Research your topic thoroughly, and continue to read around it. Being, a wide reader, is a great help because you have a better idea of the topic you need to discuss.

Preparation

Nothing can replace good planning and preparation. Analyze what you need for your speech, like visual aids. Review your speech. The more prepared you are in your speech, the more likely you will succeed in delivering it. Moreover, with sufficient preparation and, indeed, over-preparation of your material, you can concentrate on delivery.

Message

Your message should be tailored to your audience. Evaluate your message. Ask yourself these questions: - Does it teach something new to your audience that they did not know before? - Does it entertain your audience? - Does it persuade your audience to practice what you have discussed? - Does your speech share knowledge that can help people?

Language

Learn to use the appropriate words to suit your audience and occasion. Avoid using too much jargon, unless you are presenting a specific topic to a specific audience. Use simple and understandable terms. Refrain from using um's and ah's. Using these words convey lack of confidence and knowledge of your subject. Instead, pause whenever you need to recall what you need to say.

Self-confidence

By no means should you let your audience doubt your ability. You can show your confidence by looking well prepared and delivering your speech well.

Enthusiasm

A good speaker can reach out to his audience and exhibit enthusiasm in his work no matter how he feels. He shows vitality in his topics, his choice of words and his gestures. A perceptive audience can easily detect lack of interest and staleness, so make sure you can muster the enthusiasm.

Listening skills

You also need to be a good listener in order to be an effective speaker. There are three types of listening according to their purpose: - Emphatic listening - you provide emotional support to the person who is talking. - Comprehensive listening - you gather information to form an accurate conclusion or idea. Focusing on details and facts. - Critical listening - this type of listening is most useful in decision making.

Sense of self

A sense of self pertains to the way you perceive yourself. You communicate this to your audience by displaying confidence, self-assurance and assertiveness.

Integrity

Your sense of self forms your integrity. People listen to you if you have respect and confidence in conveying your message.

Sincerity

Good speakers believe in what they are saying. The ability to speak in public pays well in every part of your life, whether you are in a small group sharing opinions or delivering a speech in front of an organization. Learn the art of public speaking and you'll improve your life.

The Art Of Matching Your Speech Title To Your Speech

If you are like most of us, the next time that you are asked to give a speech, because of the importance of public speaking you'll probably spend a considerable amount of time working on the speech. You'll consider your audience, pick your words, and attempt to craft a speech that will capture their attention and allow you to get your point across. Oh, and then when you have it all put together you'll remember at the last moment that you need a title for your speech, you'll quickly think something up, and then poof you're done. However, does your speech title match your speech?

LET YOUR SPEECH TITLE GUIDE YOUR SPEECH

One of the classic questions that everyone seems to wrestle with when creating a speech is just exactly when the title for a speech should be determined: before you write the speech or afterward? It turns out the answer is before.

The reason for this is because by selecting your title before you write your speech, you can allow your speech title to guide the speech that you write. One way that you can do this is by allowing your title to determine the focus of your speech. Almost every topic that we're asked to speak about can be approached from many different ways. If you determine what approach you want to take, create a speech title that reflects this. Then as you write your speech, you'll be able to double check to make sure that your speech lines up with the title that you selected.

Some presenters use a certain type of speech called a "position" speech. These speeches have topics that your audience will either support or disagree with strongly. As the speaker, when you create the title for your speech you must choose a side. By doing this you'll find yourself giving a much better speech than if your audience was unable to determine which side your beliefs fell on.

Match The Title To The Topic

The topic that you'll be talking about is going to guide you when you are selecting a title for your speech. You'll need to consider this if you are going to want your speech to be informative, humorous, or educational? You'll want to choose a title that conveys the tone that you'll want your audience to get from your speech.

The title that you choose for your speech needs to bring your topic alive for your audience. You are going to want to make them want to hear you long before it's time for you to take the stage. One way to go about making this happen is by making your title an active title. You are going to want the title of your speech to suggest that by coming to hear you speak, your audience is going to be receiving something valuable.

Finally, the one thing that you might want to consider not doing is using clichés in your title. The reason for this is that we've all heard them so many times before that we tend to discount them: "The Keys To... ", "Secrets Of... ", etc. Understand that the first title that you think of might not be the best one. Write down the titles as they come to you and when you have a list, sit down and pick out the one that is going to best capture the imagination of your audience.

What All Of This Means For You

Long before your next audience will hear the first words out of your mouth, they'll hear your speech's title. The question for you is does your title match the content of your speech?

In order to create a fitting title that matches your speech, you need to allow your title to guide the speech that you create - this is one of the key strategies to successful public speaking. It means that your title should determine the focus of your speech and can also set the tone. If you match your title to your speech this will require you to take a position on the topic that you'll be speaking about. Make sure that your title tells the audience what you want to say about your topic.

Chapter 5: Getting To Know Yourself

Humans are social animals. Many people require social interactions with other people to lead a happy and balanced life. Humans take their social relationships very seriously- how else can we justify watching ten whole seasons of Friends? But, as Rachel, Joey and Monica demonstrate, social relationships are not easy. To make new friends, meet new partners and introduce yourself to groups in professional situations, you often need to be willing to make the first move. Even when relationships are established, they require consideration, patience, compromise and a decent amount of work to maintain them and this can feel overwhelming to people who are shy or socially anxious. One of the biggest hurdles in overcoming your shyness or anxiety and meet new people is that you first must get to know yourself. By understanding who you are and all of the things you have to offer other people, you can open up your world and move forward confidently into new social situations.

The first step in getting to know yourself and overcoming fear of social situations is understanding what triggers your feelings of shyness or anxiety. This is one of the best ways to get to know yourself in order to be able to move on with your life. There could be one or many reasons that a person might feel shy or anxious around other people. However, many people who experience shyness do so because they have a weak self-image. They feel as though they are uninteresting, unattractive and unworthy of someone else's attention when the fact is that these thoughts are entirely untrue. Sometimes, these feelings come about because at some point, someone close to you, told you that were not good enough. This can leave emotional scars that make you feel as though you are inadequate. The problem with believing the negative things that other people say is that they are not true. People often say these things to the people that they are close, because they themselves feel that way and they are projecting it onto you. When people are rude, mean or callous, they are reflecting an unhappiness with themselves off of you. When this happens, it has very little to do with you. It often means that you were just in close proximity and therefore an easy target. If you spend some time getting to know the person that you are and growing to like yourself, it will become easier to realize that the toxic things that others sometimes say are simply not true.

Another reason that some people feel like they do not fit in is because they spend so much time focusing on themselves that they over-emphasize the features about themselves that they do not like instead of focusing on the features that they do. Being preoccupied with one's self is one of the biggest reasons for insecurity. When you get caught up in using the wrong word, wearing the wrong outfit or saying the wrong to the wrong person, you may feel like you are at the center of the room and all eyes are on you. Thinking along these lines often creates a lot of unnecessary anxiety because in reality, few people will notice if you have made a mistake and fewer people will even remember because everyone is so caught up in their own insecurities that most people will forget yours in favor of their own.

Feeling like you do not fit in is the product of negative feelings that often go much deeper than you realize. But you need to be able to recognize distorted thinking so that you can diagnose it and change it. Think about the last time that you had negative feelings regarding a social situation. Were they feelings that you have had before? If so, do you think that there is a pattern in your feelings? What is it that causes you to feel this way? Often times, people can pinpoint their anxieties to a moment in time where they felt embarrassed or rejected by another person. The key is to remember that these are only our fears and while our feelings are valid; they do not always accurately represent real-life situations, especially situations that have been over-analyzed and poorly remembered.

When you decided to go down the path of self-knowledge, it can be difficult to know where to begin. But wherever you start, you must remember that you do not have to justify your worth to anyone, even yourself. Everyone is worth of respect and kindness and you should begin to show yourself the same respect and kindness that you show others. Getting to know yourself also means taking care of yourself by letting go of idealistic expectations and letting yourself grow organically. Take time for yourself to figure out what you enjoy, whether it is a solitary activity or one that requires the participation of one hundred strangers. Learning about what you enjoy and what you are good at is fun and uplifting.

Getting to know yourself is not always easy. It can bring up painful memories or unhappy moments in your life that you would rather forget. But beginning to understand who you really are is the first step on the path to beginning to realize your true worth.

Chapter 6: Practise, Rehearse And Visualize

The importance of good Practise

You've probably heard the saying practise makes perfect well in terms of public speaking this is one of the best things you can do to deliver a good speech so remember to practise. Again this may sound like common sense but it doesn't have to take a genius to understand what it takes to deliver a good speech. Regardless other than continuously practising on the stage another strategy that reduces nervousness and fear are rehearsing your speech. I should point out this is a no brainer for anything in life the more preparation and effort you put into something the more you get out of it. This applies, even more, when it comes to a speech, in all honesty, there is no limit to how much you can prepare for one but there is a line drawn between consistent practice and perfectionism. Many people do feel you need to be perfect at many things in life to be a good success but this doesn't have to be the case with a speech, regardless how much you practise it's likely you'll still mess up on the odd sentence or two if this happens don't worry about it. One of the best things to do is just keep going if you prepared for the speech and know about your subject well you can easily think of something else to talk about if you missed a point or two. By following this one method of not letting a mistake show you'll have more control in your voice and the audience. Remember your audience will only know you've made a mistake if you acknowledge and bring attention to that mistake. Certainly **do not apologize** for it either by apologizing in the middle of a speech you immediately bring attention to the part of the speech where you made a mistake. In reality, it's very likely that the audience didn't know you made the mistake or missed knew that you accidently skipped over the point you were trying to make. So don't focus on yourself, focus on the message you are trying to portray to your audience. Beginners have a habit of slipping up in their speech not because what they were presenting is bad or an uninteresting subject but because they make the mistake of focusing on themselves and not on the message they are trying to portray. By doing this you will be less anxious during the speech and will bring less attention to any mistake you do make and this will just propel the rest of your speech to a higher level with more quality because you are not concerned that you are making mistakes. Think about it if you were focusing primarily on yourself and just attempting to not make any mistakes then when you do make one that will just bug you for the rest of the speech which will show off in the quality of the rest of your presentation. Whereas if you focus just on the message and with getting the audience to participate on the message in your mind you won't realize if you're making mistakes or not, or maybe you will realize but it won't concern you and you'll be able to follow through easily because you're not concerned. Advanced speakers know how to guide the audience's attention towards what's important about the presentation and away from the small errors. Whether you make a mistake or not just remember that people want you to do well and because of that they are rooting for you.

Become an authority on your subject

Another way to avoid nervousness when communicating to an audience is by being an authority on the subject you are discussing. There are some logistics involved and certain things you ought to do to tailor your speech but if the audience knows you are an authority on the subject you are discussing then they will want to know and learn all they can from you. Being an authority on the subject means you have power and power usually breeds confidence, so if there is something that excites you this is the thing you can talk about to an audience. Therefore, rehearse the speech and keep discussing it. If you do this long enough on the public stage, eventually with enough practise and dedication you'll become an authority on that subject and this way you'll find it much easier to become a competent speaker. If you believe you can't do this, then just remember this quote preached by Tony Robins "what you focus on expands" so basically the more you focus on something the more that thing will expand. Focus on the skills you want to improve your voice tonality, eye contact, your posture, and enthusiasm, remember 93% of your communication is body language so focus on what's weakest for you. If you have the goal of becoming an authority on a subject, you can use your mind to focus on what it is you want we will go further into this in the next section.

Visualize

So how do you focus on something? By using your mind just think about the thing you want improvement in, this is a key part of the successful preparation and it's known as visualization. Visualize yourself already giving that good speech and soon enough you'll be living the reality of it. Remember to include all aspects of the speech when visualizing so that means to imagine a good opener, think about your audience being captivated by what you're saying, think about adding in good pauses to allow your audience to applaud and absorb what you are explaining and, of course, visualize yourself finishing strong. By doing this it counts as a significant part of rehearsing so don't just write rewrite and say your speech out loud when rehearsing but also take the time to visualize your speech. Now, this may seem like a large task but if there is an important speech coming up just take 15 minutes out of your day to visualize yourself giving a successful speech. If you do that then it's just eliminating the chance of your speech going poorly or seeing any of those mistakes you fear from manifesting. In fact, the opposite will be true the more you visualize the more likely the speech will be a success and go even better than expected. Try this out and you can be the judge of whether it makes the difference.

Know your audience

Another way to get a good response from the audience is by knowing who you are presenting to so be aware of the geography of people. Have you taken a trip to the capital or the other side of the country to deliver a speech? Or have you gone further say to a different country? Well, realize depending how far you travel people's culture, attitudes (especially political ones) can be very different from where you've come from. Be aware of this during your presentation. More importantly, however, you can use this to play to your advantage. For example, where ever comedians do their shows they often incorporate some jokes about where they are and most of the time this will bring laughter from the audience and relax them moving forward. When you have an audience and you do this it will help relax and put and your audience at ease not to mention it will bring more fluidity to your speech. If you have a research project from university, then if you are presenting to a group of students and professors then feel free to use complex language. However, if you are doing this to a bunch of say high school students then you will need to tailor your language to that audience so they understand what you're talking about. Just keep this in mind when presenting by knowing the age, culture, political orientation and geography of the group then this will help relax you in the delivery of the speech.

Practicalities of your venue

When preparing a speech remember not to forget to think about the venue you are presenting in. Are you presenting via PowerPoint? If you have, have you considered the fact that there may not be a projector screen or monitor you can present from? Today it's more likely that yes venues will have these but you can never assume if you've never been to that location before so be sure to check on this. How big is your audience? If you are presenting to 50+ people it may be wise to see whether any speakers are available to help carry your voice you don't want to be shouting continuously just to make sure everybody hears you by doing this, you'll save a lot of unnecessary stress down the road and on the day of your presentation. If the venue is big and has a lot of windows beams of sunlight could come through obstructing the audience's view of your PowerPoint. So make sure these windows are covered or that there are curtains/blinds at the venue. Small details like this will reduce your stress even more and allow you presentation to go even more smoothly.

Death by PowerPoint

The saying "death by PowerPoint" is certainly renowned in education and business meetings. So obviously, you want to avoid this problem. One thing you could do is increase how visual your PowerPoint presentation is. PowerPoints are commonly formatted in paragraph style or listed bullet point style and this can often turn the audience off from what you're saying. I'm not saying to take all writing out of the PowerPoint but expand on the visuals as this will go a long way to maintaining the attention of your audience. Also, make sure you don't read bullet points out word for word this surely will turn off your audience so just write pointers not entire sentences on the PowerPoint or the paper and rehearse the details. If you hold eye, contact and speak from your head more people will be more willing to stay present and focus on what you got to say. The parts you should be rehearsing the most are those that you struggle remembering just keep going over these points and they will no longer be your weakest points of the speech. This all comes back to good preparation and whether you present to a large extent or not by doing all this you will not feel so nervous and may even feel a sense of confidence about the speech before you start! If this is the case for you then this will definitely show off in the delivery and it won't tune out the audience but rather keep them engaged. I hope these concepts help you deliver a good speech. The most important thing here is not what you've learnt but what you have done to apply this information, by applying the pointers expressed here your speech very likely will turn into good one. However, if you don't apply anything you've read here then this information is next to useless, the application is the key word to remember here.

Chapter 7: Build Your Confidence

Nobody is born with limitless self-confidence. If someone seems to have incredible self-confidence, it's because he or she has worked on building it for years. Self-confidence is something that you learn to build up because the challenging world of business and life in general, can deflate it.

Here are some secrets you can use to build up your self-confidence as a Speaker.

Meditate

If you're frustrated and depressed because of things that happened in the past and nothing worked to change your feelings towards it, you need to start meditating. Find stillness, remain calm and take long breathes. With meditation, you get to keep yourself away from the busy and fast-paced noisy world. You keep yourself away from distractions and make yourself at ease with meditation.

Identify Yourself and Find Your Source of Shyness

Each person experiences his or her shyness in a unique way or identity, so you have to, first of all, identify yourself and understand what situations trigger this feeling of fear or shyness and why? For example, do you have stomach pains when you are asked to speak in public or do you feel shy or nervous when speaking to a large group of people for the first time? When you are able to identify yourself and understand yourself and your source of shyness, you can now begin to overcome your shyness by examining the nature of your fear or shyness and practicing to overcome it.

Start With Very, Very Small Talk and Simple Actions:

Get your feet wet. Shy people often report that they have trouble talking with people they have just met, particularly those people to whom they might feel attracted. A strategy for helping shy people to overcome this inhibition is to start with relatively non-threatening situations and very small talk. Non-threatening situations might include malls, museums, political rallies, or sporting events where you will have the opportunity to interact with a lot of people for a relatively brief period of time. In such interactions, you can start by smiling and saying something simple like "hello" to as many people as you care to make eye contact with and who will smile at you. Asking for simple directions, giving an unexpected compliment, or offering assistance (e.g., offer to hold a door) are three very simple ways to practice talking with people. Thus, the point here is to get used to talking with others.

Develop Conversation Skills: How To Keep Talking.

Shy people who have mastered the art of small talk can take the next step by developing their conversational skills. The trick to a successful conversation is to have something to say. There are a number of very simple strategies that shy people can employ to make sure they have something to say. You can start by reading the newspaper or magazines and/or listening to information-based radio programs. The advantage of such information sources is that they also give you the type of in-depth, "behind-the-headlines" analysis that is the basic substance of much social conversation. Shy people can also do their part to help keep the conversation going by asking open-ended questions that require more than a yes or no answer (e.g., What do you think of . . . ?).

Come To Terms with Audience Expressions

Your anxiety level is increased when you misinterpret the audience's facial expression. In normal conversation, we're accustomed to getting feedback from the listener—a nod or a smile here and there that signal approval. But when we present, audiences listen differently. They're more likely to give the speaker a blank stare, which doesn't mean they don't like what they hear; more often than not, it simply means they're concentrating on the message. This is especially true of audience members who are introverted.

Become an Expert on Your Topic

You will greatly increase your confidence and success as a public speaker by thoroughly researching your topic. What you present in your speech comprises only a small portion of what you know about the topic. If you don't do your research, you will be nervous about your speech.

Learn To Take Rejection: No One Is Liked By Everyone.

Rejection is one of the risks that accompany engaging in social interactions. A key to overcoming shyness is not to take rejection personally. There may be a variety of reasons that someone is rejected by someone else, none of which may have anything at all to do with the person being rejected. For example, one person may not like what the shy person is wearing, and another person may be bored with the entire social situation, not just with her conversation with the shy individual. The point is that sometimes you can control the reactions of others (e.g., by wearing stylish clothes) and at other times you cannot. What's important is that shy people make a realistic attempt to socialize with others.

Find Your Comfort Zone: Do What Fits You.

Not all social situations are for everyone. For example, some shy people might be uneasy in a bar or nightclub where physical attractiveness and stylish dress are critical predictors of social success. In other situations, extensive knowledge of politics, art, or murder mysteries might be the key to success. Shy people should seek out those situations that are most consistent with their temperament and interests. It is easier for shy people to overcome or manage their sense of social anxiety and self-consciousness by finding situations in which they feel reasonably comfortable. Volunteering for different organizations is a good strategy for shy people to use in an attempt to find various places where they might feel comfortable. In most cases, being a volunteer requires a low level of skills, offers the possibility of meeting many different types of people, and is easy to terminate if the experience does not turn out to be what was expected. Thus, overcoming shyness can be helped by seeking out an assortment of volunteer experiences as a means of meeting new people, practicing social skills in different situations, and helping to find those social situations that are the most comfortable

Practice As If You're the Worst

When you know your material well, there's a tendency to get sloppy when practicing a speech: You might flip through the slides, mentally thinking about what you are going to say, without actually rehearsing out loud exactly what you plan to say. This results in a presentation that's not as sharp as it could be and might cause you to be nervous once you have 100 pairs of eyes staring at you.

Focus on Your Message, Not on Your Fear

The more you think about being anxious about speaking, the more you will increase your level of anxiety. Instead, in the few minutes before you speak, mentally review your major ideas, your introduction, and your conclusion. Focus on your ideas rather than on your fear.

Visualize Your Success

Imagine yourself giving your speech. Picture yourself walking confidently to the front and delivering your well prepared opening remarks. Visualize yourself giving the entire speech as a controlled, confident speaker. Imagine yourself calm and in command.

Practice Breathing Exercises

Proper breathing technique is fundamental to having a strong, confident speaking voice. Performing some simple exercises will help you to project your sound and maintain a relaxed manner while speaking. Breathing exercises are particularly useful when you are preparing to speak in front of a group.

Body Posture

In order to breathe properly, you must stand in a posture that facilitates deep inhalation and exhalation. Stand with your feet nearly shoulder-width apart, distributing your weight on both balls of your feet and your heels. With each exhalation, release tension in your shoulders and relax your neck and jaws.

Exaggerated Movement Exercise

A relaxed jaw and throat facilitate deep breathing. Rosemary Scott Vohs, storytelling and speech communication instructor at Western Washington University, suggests making some exaggerated movements with your face to ease tension in the jaw and open the throat. First, lift the eyebrows and open the mouth wide. Then, yawn widely and loudly, saying "yah, yah, yah." Stretch your mouth, saying "see, ooo, eee, ooo," in an exaggerated fashion.

Know Your Introduction and Conclusion Well

Successfully presenting the introduction of your speech will boost your confidence, help calm your nerves, and reduce worrisome thoughts that increase anxiety. Knowing that you'll finish with a coherent, smooth, and memorable conclusion will increase your confidence and lessen your nervousness throughout your speech. One useful strategy for knowing your introduction and conclusion well is to write them out word for word. Then read them aloud a few times, listening to how they sound and making any necessary changes. Once you're satisfied with your introduction and conclusion, commit them to memory as best you can. Although generally, you don't want to memorize your entire speech, memorizing your introduction and conclusion will help you present them more fluently and lessen your anxiety.

Chapter 8: Your Signature Look

As a TV/radio presenter, you represent the TV network/ radio station you work for. As a public speaker you represent the organisation or community you speak for. Whatever the look you decide to go in for, and whatever you put on, it will mirror not only your image and style, but also a certain image of the network or organization you're working for.

A TV presenter is as important as the logo of the TV network he or she works for. The presenter is even more important for the simple reason that the logo takes up only about 5 per cent of the screen, while a TV presenter covers about 60 per cent of the screen. And while scanning channels, audiences rapidly identify the TV channel by its TV presenter, even before getting the time to look at the logo. Therefore, while the TV station works on its logo only once to make it project its best image, you have to work on your looks every day to keep looking your best.

1. Public figure

Now that you're regularly going on TV/radio, or on a podium as a public speaker, you might as well choose for yourself an appealing image that sets you apart from the commonplace. A self-image that makes you, as a public figure, impress your audience and therefore leave a positive impression and remain in their memory, as a person as well as the content you're delivering.

Nevertheless, as a TV presenter, you might, later on, leave your TV network for another. During the process of job hunting on other networks, you won't be applying as a TV presenter regardless of your image and looks. In fact, you will be submitting this self-image as a public figure to be part of the new TV network you're trying to join. And this image is part of what will get you appointed. This is why it is extremely important to build for yourself a signature image that is loved and familiar to as wide a range of audiences as possible.

As a TV presenter, not only do you represent the TV station you work for, you represent yourself as a public figure. At this first stage of your career, you'll have to work hard to build your signature image. Furthermore, every time you go on TV, you will be promoting yourself, marketing your self-image and preparing yourself to be presented to viewers as a personality, independently of any TV network or radio station you might work for.

2. Looks

There's the classic look, the fashionable look, and there's something in between. Whatever is the look you choose, it will become your 'signature look'.

Observe your looks - clothes, hair, make-up, accessories... Monitor what looks good on you, and what doesn't; what generates positive feedback, and what doesn't. Try to find something that can specifically give your image this 'special something', this special 'signature look' that we're talking about. It could be some kind of accessory, a specific style of watch, a hairstyle or hair color, eye make-up. any specific fashion that you find yourself effortlessly going for every time you go on TV, or on a public-speaking podium. Any fashion which makes you feel content about your image, and generates positive audience feedback about you as well, will do. It's something that your audience will notice every time they see you. And they will naturally get used to seeing you with that look and look forward to checking it every time they come back to watch you.

However, don't be hard on yourself if you don't find your signature look that easily. It's not that simple to do this on your own. Most TV presenters and public figures hire a marketing and image make-over consultant to do that for them. Some TV networks might hire someone for you. If that's not the case for you, and since you're still at the beginning of your career, and you might not be able to afford it, you can still do it on your own, as long as you keep it simple and don't go in for the extreme fashion trends. Viewers might have different opinions about eccentric fashion trends, but they all happen to accept a classic and simple style. I will walk you through the 'How to do it on your own' hereafter.

3- How to create your signature image without getting any professional help

A public speaker and/or anchor communicates to his audience through his dress code. And just like there's a dress code appropriate for every occasion, there's a dress code appropriate to each kind of speech and/or TV programme.

A motivational public speaker can choose vibrant colours, a management consultant public speaker chooses a formal suit, while a meditation mentor public speaker goes in for white or beige cotton pants and shirt....

While a news anchor is apt to dress formally, an entertainment show presenter or a fashion show presenter can benefit from a broader range of options. However, whatever the programme you are presenting, and no matter how formal, there's still a lot that you can do with your style and image.

A - Choosing your 'special something'

Pick something small, a delicate addition to your style, but which can become, with time, your 'special something', your 'image signature'. Don't choose something eccentric, neither something very old-fashioned. It has to be a simple fashion trend, or a fashionably classic one.

You can choose to tie a scarf stylishly around the neck (a trend chosen by actress Jennifer Aniston lately). It

could be your hairstyle: your hair forehead fringe, or your hair colour. Try to go for a redhead, a platinum blonde, or a blue black, if it looks good on you, for example. However, a signature style will accompany you throughout your career; it's not something you can change every other month (unless you choose having a new style every month as your signature image, which is actually a good idea if you present a fashion show programme). So if you decide to go in for a special hairstyle, try to choose something that really goes well with your face shape and skin tone. And try to choose something you can live with for a long period of time, not the kind of colour or hairstyle you feel you'll get bored of within a couple of months.

You can choose to be creative with your accessories - a specific style of necklaces, for example, or earrings. This also can be your signature image. Male news anchors, for instance, can decide to carefully choose their watch collection; they can go in for big-size, square leather watches. As for male daytime TV presenters, they can get as creative as the ladies TV presenters.

Finally, your signature image can be your posture, and a gesture you make repeatedly during your programme. However, don't try a new gesture or posture on purpose, as you might risk looking odd. Remember to take your time. All these looks-related issues have to come naturally. Don't rush into anything you might regret later. Give yourself time and monitor your style over the days. And your 'signature image' will find the light on its own soon - all you have to do is take notice of it and embrace it.

B. Keeping it neutral

What does keeping your looks neutral mean? And why exactly should you keep it neutral?

A neutral look means an impartial look, a look that doesn't insinuate any religious, political, social, or any other kind of commitment to a specific group of people. This is because belonging to a specific group of people, from a religious, political or social point of view, explicitly insinuates that you favour this group of people over the rest. You are a public figure and that means that you should keep your personal beliefs to yourself. You maintain the right to practise them during your own time. However, when you're working, you belong to the public. And your looks actually affect the organisation or TV/Radio network you're working for. Anything that suggests your belonging to a specific community will insinuate that the organisation or TV/Radio favours this community as well over the other groups of audiences. And this is harmful for an organisation, or a TV/ Radio network that normally wants to reach the widest possible number of audiences. On the other hand, if the organization or TV/ Radio network clearly states its religious or political beliefs, then whatever your personal beliefs are, you will most probably be automatically categorised as having the same beliefs as those of your organization/ network. Only then can you wear something that might state your commitment to the religion, political group, or community to which the network subscribes without getting either the network or the audience irritated. Since in that case, it will be OK for the organization or TV/Radio station to express your beliefs as well as for the audience, who will mainly be from the same community and therefore espouse the same religious, political, or social point of view.

Remember that you mirror the beliefs and commitments of the TV/radio network / organization that you work for, so unless the organization in question is committed to something, you shouldn't manifest your personal beliefs through the way you look, dress and accessorise.

That doesn't mean that you should desist from fighting for some of your beliefs throughout your work as a TV/radio journalist or public speaker; otherwise you will be missing the whole point of being a journalist and public speaker. However, when you want to fight for an issue, and make it your personal battle, let it be an issue that galvanises all viewers, no matter what country, religion or political party they belong to. For example, you may embrace a humanitarian cause, get vocal about a human rights violation, and fight for the encouragement of new artistic talent that haven't yet had the opportunity to get into the spotlight. You may commit to any cause that bring together people from around the globe, and avoid any other that leads people to fight, make war, and harm one another. As far as your other personal beliefs are concerned, no one has the right to deny you them, but just check them at home before you go to work, in order to be able to deliver something pleasant for all viewers out there, no matter what their beliefs are.

Chapter 9: Where Do I Begin When Crafting Messages That Matter?

Leaders are inundated with questions continuously. Some are complex and some are not. The messages that matter are often routine answers for questions that are always asked of the leader. When I sit down with a leader or executive and ask him or her to list the most common questions asked, the most difficult questions asked, or, the most important questions asked, the leader or executive can usually list them quickly.

These are the questions or issues leaders must answer based on who they are, what they are about, and where they learned the answer. It requires work to develop a two-minute, twelve-minute, and twenty-minute answer for these important questions. The two-minute answer is the one given to constituents or patrons, the twelve-minute is a Rotary or Chamber of

Commerce presentation, and the twenty-minute speech is a Policy Presentation or similar educationally-focused presentation.

My routine answers are based on "Who Am I?" And What I Am About—the rules for life I believe in. The first two aspects of the answer are illustrated with the story of the person or events that instilled the first two elements in my life. Who you are doesn't change and your core belief that drives the answer to the question doesn't change, what changes are the stories to illustrate W1| "Who Am I?" and W2| "What Am I About?" This is true whether you are a Chief Executive Officer or a politician developing stump speeches and preparing for a question-and-answer session on the issues. Because there are similarities between being the leader of an organization and a politician campaigning for a seat, this section deals with them interchangeably.

When I work with executives and politicians asked to repeatedly respond on the same issues, we develop storyboards for these issues that include the same W1| "Who Am I?" two or three variations on statements of W2| "What Am I About?" and multiple stories in W3| "Where did you learn that?" which illustrate the core belief. The simple formula is: "Who Am I?" followed by a statement of the rule based on "What am I about?" Who am I, doesn't change. The same rule may be stated in different perspectives and changes to reflect a response to a question. This is because the rule ("What you are about?") is almost always a rule answering a question or resolving a dilemma.

Think in this way: A W2 (What Are You About?) will be a statement or rule in response to issues you routinely face in life, questions you are asked, questions that challenge your belief about "Who Are You?"

Here is the question facing a diminutive black woman in Montgomery, Alabama, who worked as a seamstress for a local department store. The question she faced involved racial inequality requiring "coloreds" to ride in the back of the bus. The Declaration of Independence states a profound W1:

W1: Who are we?

"All men are created equal they are endowed by their Creator with certain unalienable Rights, that among these are Life, Liberty and the pursuit of Happiness."

W2: What am I about?

Sometimes standing up for justice means holding your seat on the bus. Or an alternative, "Justice denied anywhere diminishes justice everywhere." (Martin Luther King Jr.)

W3: Where did I learn that?

After working a full day as a seamstress at the Montgomery Fair department store, Rosa Parks boarded the Cleveland Avenue bus at 6:00 PM December 1, 1955. She sat in the first row of the colored seats reserved for black riders. The seats reserved for white riders filled as the bus traveled its route and when it reached the third stop along the way in front of the Empire Theater several more white passengers boarded.

The bus driver stepped to the back of the bus and moved the colored section sign several rows back behind Rosa, expecting her to stand and allow the white men to sit. The driver asked why she didn't stand and allow the white men to sit and she told him she didn't think she should have to stand up. The driver called the police and she was arrested.

So began the boycott of buses in Montgomery, Alabama, that resulted in the equal civil rights of all African American citizens to ride in freedom. Sometimes standing up for justice means holding your seat on the bus, or the alternative, "Justice denied anywhere diminishes justice everywhere."

The great controversies of life involve questions that challenge our personal philosophy. How we answer those questions determines our success or failure in life. When you think of individuals whose actions turned the course of human history, you realize that they were not afraid to answer the question and be in conflict with the status quo. They knew who they were, and what they were about.

My personal experiences include being an executive in a large public school system and having to deal with the prickly issues that come up regularly. As a trial attorney, I have to craft an accurate message that will resonate with a jury or judge. As a world champion of public speaking, I have been asked to coach executives and candidates in preparing speeches and developing speaking skills for critical events. In each of these different scenarios, I begin the process with a question that frames the issue.

You must first understand the question. It is human nature to interpret a question as being the precedent to the answer we want to answer. This is akin to Henry

Ford's answer to the question, What color Model T can I get? The answer: "Any customer can have a car painted any color that he wants, so long as it is black." 12 The power of leadership is the ability to frame the question and then provide an answer that moves people toward an outcome. Think carefully what question you want to answer! Framing the issue, frames the answer.

Framing the question is not always possible. You can, however, manage the question to strategically answer the question you want to answer. Reporters ask provocative questions to get provocative answers. Astute politicians answer the question they want to answer no matter what question was asked by the reporter. That isn't always possible if you are a school superintendent responding to a school board inquiry or a driver responding to a patrol officer about your speed; it may be difficult to reframe the question. Answering prickly-pointed questions is outside the scope of this book. What I will develop for you is a strategy for analyzing the prickly questions that come up in your profession and teach you how to develop meaningful answers you can present in a formidable way.

It is a simple process of listing all the questions you will be asked, have been asked, or might be asked. On a yellow pad or a piece of butcher paper, put each prickly question at the top of the page. Then ask yourself the three questions:

1. In relation to this issue "Who am I?" What is my underlying conviction and philosophy;

2. What am I about? If I could answer this question in one sentence, what would that sentence be? And finally,

3. What is my personal story from which I draw my understanding and conviction about this question? What is the first story that comes to my mind related to this topic?

Initially, you want to free-write everything you can think about in response to these three questions. Once you have done that, set it aside for a day or two, then come back to it with a clear head and eyes to look it over. Pare it down to as few words as you need to state it completely. Using the statement will become natural as you work through it.

Cites for Chapter:

12. Remark about the Model T in 1909, published in his autobiography My Life and Work (1922) Chapter IV [p. 71–72].

Chapter 10: Assessment

After the meticulous study of your material, it is important to practice its delivery. When practicing a speech, you need honest sources of feedback to know your areas of improvement. Do not take criticism personally. Remember that these statements' purpose is to make you a better performer and save you from the embarrassment of the actual staging.

Feedback can come in first person or third person. Your family or relatives, friends or even professionals in this field can help. There is no shame in looking for a coach when it comes to public speaking; even experts themselves advise it. Next is you yourself! You can practice facing a mirror or on any elevated flat surface to serve as your stage. If possible, it is highly recommended to invest in a video recorder with good audio pickups.

With a recording device, you can review your postures, gestures and voice. The way we move is a form of statement. It is even reported that non-verbal communication is a stronger indicator of our true message than mere words. A classic example: when someone is blinking a lot or cannot look you in the eye while he's saying something, he's probably lying.

Your voice too should be carefully assessed as for tonality, pronunciation, pace, pitch and volume. Never try to imitate your favorite speaker's voice. Take note of this because sometimes we tend to unconsciously mimic our role models. Be natural and use your own voice. Imitating someone adds unnecessary effort and will make you sound awkward.

Listen carefully to your tone. Avoid having a single tone (i.e. sounding like a robot). As a speaker, from the root word itself, speak; your pronunciation should be clear. When you listen to your recording, be conscious of your pace as well. If you speak too fast, you'll mumble. And if you speak too slowly, you'll only lull your audience to sleep.

Be mindful of the time too during practice. The last thing you want is to be pressured by a ticking clock. Likewise, nobody wants to sit through an event with an exaggerated timespan. Make use of a timer and adjust your piece to the desired time length.

Chapter 11: Steps Of How To Control Yourself

You are the show.

When you make a presentation about something, people watch you. You are the show not the PowerPoint presentation or the visual aids. The pleasure comes from your side. People go to watch movies in theaters because of the movie stars themselves not the movie story.

People would be interested in the public speech presentation you are giving because of you not other things.

So, invest in your time because you are the show itself.

Add a value.

If you are going to make a presentation, you should add a value to your audience. If no adding value, don't make the presentation. People will not be interested if they already know the information.

No add value = No presentation.

Never apologize.

At the beginning of the presentation and under any personal excuse, never apologize like "I want to apologize for you! I didn't sleep well yesterday! "Or "I am sorry I didn't prepare the presentation slides well because I didn't have enough time this week ". This will destroy your presentation and will leave bad and negative impression on you throughout the presentation.

Remember you are the show. Presentation slides are just an aiding tool that you can present without them.

Take care of "FIRST SIX WORDS" rule.

This rule says that the first six words you begin your speech with give the audience long lasting impression on your presentation.

If you began the speech with low volume or a lazy tone or hesitating tone, people will take a negative impression and you will lose audience interest and attention over the presentation.

If you started with strong tone and enthusiastic beginning, audience will be very interested and will focus with you all the presentation duration.

Some people say it is also called "FIRST SIX INCHES" rule as it is the first top 6 inches of your body (including face, neck and part of your chest). If you are well dressed and showed enthusiasm with your face impressions and your gesture, people will get along with you (and vice versa).

Exploit your body talk and gestures to deliver the message

Body language is more effective than speaking only when you are sending your message.

Studies showed that 55% of your message would be interpreted or perceived by the receiver through your body language. 40%

would be interpreted according to your voice tone .Only 5 % for your words.

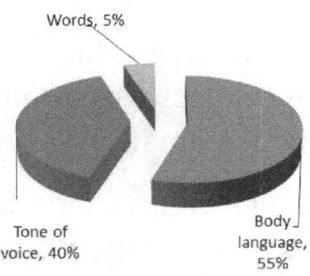

Use your body language in situation of feelings:

When you present sad situation, you should feel sad (no smiling).

When you present happy situation, you should smile.

Use suitable tone in your speech:

Raise your voice in important situations (like making a **bold** word in a paragraph to show the importance of the word).

When you meet somebody and speaks to him with your feelings is better for message communications than speaking to him through the phone.

Speaking to somebody through the phone is better for message communications than sending him email.

Words communication method like (email or text messages) is very poor method to deliver the information as it doesn't contain any feelings or the importance tone for the message.

Make sure that your gestures match the situation you are presenting.

Don't say "UM"s

Some presenters always say "UM..UM..UM "when they think while speaking. This often distracts the audience attention.

You can make silent pause instead. It will be more effective in the presentation. It also needs training and preparation.

Choose your display words.

In PowerPoint data show, don't put every word in the presentation slides. Audience doesn't have to read every single word, but rather put the keywords to allow you to display the subject.

Do you think this flooded slide will be useful for the audience?

World electricity consumption down in 2009

- At the world level, energy consumption was cut down by 1.5% during 2009, for the first time since World War II. Except in Asia and Middle East, consumptions were reduced in all the world regions. In OECD countries, accounting for 53% of the total, electricity demand scaled down by more than 4.5% in both Europe and North America while it shrank by above 7% in Japan. Electricity demand also dropped by more than 4.5% in CIS countries, driven by a large cut in Russian consumption. Conversely, in China and India (22% of the world's consumption), electricity consumption continued to rise at a strong pace (+6-7%) to meet energy demand related to high economic growth. In Middle East, growth rate was softened but remained high, just below 4%

Of course not!! But if you put it in the slide simple keywords like the following picture, it will be more useful and you will present the subject:

World electricity consumption down in 2009

- In 2009 cut down by 1.5% .
- In OECD countries, down by more than 4.5%
- In CIS countries Electricity demand dropped by 4.5%
- China and India increased (+6-7%)

(This is only for show not a real figures)

Check your words' spelling.

In PowerPoint presentation never put wrong words spelling. Check your sentences grammar. Use bullets in your points but not more than 6 bullets in one slide.

Make Editions for your presentation according to audience ages and wants.

Giving a presentation of certain subject to a 20 years old audience is totally different from giving presentation to a 60 years audience even it is the same subject.

You should speak to each audience with his language, style, thinking and mentality. So you will prepare and edition for the presentation for each audience. If the same edition used, one of them will not get the message of the presentation.

Example:

If you are giving a sales presentation to sell a new car!

For the audience of 60 years old: You will present that the car has very comfortable luxury seats, the car has a self parking option ….etc.

For the audience of 20 years old: You will present that the car has "Bluetooth calling while driving option", the car has back seats DVD monitors, Ability to play station connections …etc.

This is how you grape audience attention.

Include stories in your presentation

You may mention real stories in your presentation to support your idea.

Use your own life stories if possible (it will be more convincing to the audience). Use the end of the story to tie it back to your presentation topic.

The story should be short (not to deviate from the presentation)

Include humor in your presentation

When you feel that your presentation became boring, you should give a break or include some humor to the presentation to get the audience attention back to your presentation.

The humor should be respectable and short.

Try to plan your stories & humor and use the one which worked before.

Chapter 12: On Getting A Love Life

If you find it hard to handle social situations and you constantly avoid going out, you will never have the chance to interact with other people. And, this would greatly affect your love life. Being an introvert does not mean you are to live alone for the rest of your life. Therefore, you should get out of your shell and see the world and it endless possibilities. This also means that you have to assess your strengths and incorporate them in your dating strategies.

Now, the next big question is where to search. You may try out the following:

Online Dating

This is getting more popular these days as it offers a more convenient way to meet new people and prospective partners in life. You are able to choose whom to chat with because all you have to do is check a person's profile page to get to know more about his fields of interests. It is much simpler than taking chances to meet Mr. or Ms. Right on your way to the cafeteria, mall or a bar.

Attending classes

Enrolling in a class is a great way to meet new people who share the same interests as you do. Having shared interests bridges interesting conversations. As an introvert, you will not be afraid to speak up because you know very well that you are to get a positive feedback.

Become a volunteer

If you love giving service to your community, you should give volunteering a try. As an introvert, this is deemed as one of the best ways to socialize and get to know new people. There are a lot of possibilities to meet someone who could turn out to be THE ONE.

Choose the right place to date

Say you have already found someone, so what would be your next move? On a date, of course! In choosing a place to go on for a date, noisy places like bars and overcrowded spots are definitely not a good place because you cannot have sound conversations there. Instead, you may choose coffeehouses, art museums or art galleries as ideal places for a first meet-up.

General Dating Tips for Introverts

No pretentions – There is nothing wrong with being an introvert. It is not a communicable disease to be ashamed of. If you are an introvert, show it. At first, people may have something to say about you – or suspect that something is wrong with you. But in the long run, they will understand you. Just be yourself and do not pretend to be someone you are not.

Don't make labels distract you - People tend to generalize and say that introverts are for introverts. This somehow limits you to have a broader dating option, but don't concentrate on this kind of belief. Remember that there is also a belief proved by Science that opposite poles attract. If you suddenly fell for an extrovert, and you couldn't just imagine yourself being with that special someone in big crowds, don't lose hope thinking that you will never have the chance to have a wonderful relationship.

The solution to the problem is mutual regard and to try to understand each other. An extrovert who understands an introvert partner who would like to recharge after a long acquaintance and give him the space he needed is someone worthy to live with. On the other hand, an introvert partner can reach out to an extrovert partner for their need to socialize by accompanying his/her partner to a social gathering or event.

Chapter 13: Organizing And Outlining

It's time to move on to the double-O's. Organizing and outlining your speech.

In this phase, we transition from thinking about the overall context and environment of where you'll be speaking and we get into the actual building and construction of what you're going to say. The meat and potatoes. The bread and butter. The rice and beans.

Well, you get the idea. This is the really important part.

Whether you are delivering a 60 second introduction at a business dinner or a 60 minute keynote speech at a convention, going through each of these phases will help you craft your message and feel more confident and prepared when you finally stand up in front of a crowd.

A. Researching

In order to get yourself in the right frame of mind, first put together an objective statement that expresses the point that you wish to achieve from your overall presentation.

You do have a point to make, don't you?

No matter how long or how short the presentation is, your objective statement will always remain the same. It is the solution to the enquiry, "Who are my audience, and what effect can my speech make on them?"

As you get an idea of what you want to achieve from your speech, you can now start doing your research.

If you are not already an authoritative expert on your topic, do the necessary reading and be sure to ask questions if you do not have sufficient information.

B. Organizing

Once your research is completed, move on to compiling. This is where the raw clay begins to get lumped and formed together.

Make any cuts as needed, you can probably pare down a good bit of information that is not entirely relevant. This is where knowing something about your audience is vital. Try to put yourself in the place of someone who will be listening to your speech. Is the information you've collected relevant for them? Is it too basic? Too advanced? Use your best judgement and don't be afraid to drop content from your speech that you don't feel 100% comfortable with.

Now is also a good time to double-check any facts, statistics or other points. From this point forward, you must have complete confidence in the accuracy of the material you've collected.
C.Ordering&Outlining

Reading a prepared speech from a piece of paper will make for an extremely tedious experience for your audience. Don't write your speech – outline it on 3x5 index cards.

Not only will your delivery sound more nature and fluid, but your practice sessions will be significantly easier. Using notecards, you can rearrange and reorder your speech with ease during the practice phase.

If you have trouble creating an outline, feel free to write your speech down and then condense it into bullet points for the notecards.

Work on the outline, refining your work repetitiously until it becomes a polished gem. The more revisions you go through, the more you'll become acquainted with your material.

Our eventual goal is to get to the point where your innate knowledge about the presentation will become so strong that you'll be able to easily go through the complete speech without even needing to reference these cards.

When I have created note cards for use on stage, I have often used a 2-in-1 approach to encourage more natural-sounding speech. Here's how I do it, but feel free to use whatever method works best for you.

WHAT I WANT TO SAY: "GlobalTech is a leading innovator in the production of widgets. Our profits have soared through the roof since we introduced the Widget4000, which has taken the entire product line to a whole new level. We are now dominating the marketplace, with annual sales growth of 22%."

WHAT I WRITE ON THE FRONT OF THE CARD:
* Innovator
* Profits Up
* Sales 22%

WHAT I WRITE ON THE BACK OF THE CARD:
* Leading Innovator in Widgets
* Widget4000 Causes Profits to Soar
* Dominating Market – Sales Up 22%

As you can see in the above examples, my notecard contains two versions of the same thing – a trio of condensed talking points.

I find that three points is the maximum I can fit on a card and still comfortably glance down to read it. My goal is to always use the more abbreviated front of the notecard for quick reference and to trigger my brain and help keep me on track. This works fantastic as a safety net if you've already gotten your speech down pat and you just need something to help jog your memory a bit.

If you are not as confident in your preparation and find yourself struggling with the shorter bullet points, simply turn the card over for a more complete series of notes.

Why bother with this? Well, it's to give yourself options and to help you study.

Using shorter bullet points that are written in larger font will make your reliance on the cards less obvious to the audience and your speech pattern will seem more natural. If you revert to using the more extensive notes on the back of the cards, you'll spend slightly more time looking down and reading your notes and your delivery will begin to sound more scripted.

Having both sets of notes can also be a huge help in studying your speech. They become flash cards to help you train. If you're writing up notecards right before your speech, you're doing it wrong. These cards should, ideally, be prepared as early as possible so that you can practice with them.

Run through the speech in your mind over and over again using the shorter notes on the front of your cards. If you run into a mental block, flip them over for reference.

Chapter 14: The Types Of Speech

Before you begin writing and delivering speeches, you must have a good grasp of the different types of speeches. All the speeches that are tackled in this chapter can be applied to public speaking, thus it is necessary that you familiarize yourself with them.

The Two Main Types of Speeches

There are two main types of speeches. The first type is called the impromptu or extemporaneous speech, while the second type is called the planned or deliberate speech.

Impromptu or Extemporaneous Speeches

These speeches are hastily prepared for. These are the kind of speech that test your wit and knowledge on how to stand in front of a crowd and deliver a speech that they will remember, even without the aid of notecards. Impromptu speeches are usually the ones that are delivered for competitions in academic institutions. However, in the professional world, impromptu speeches can range from delivering important announcements, engaging in sudden public relations functions, or giving a toast for a dear friend.

Planned or Deliberate Speeches

In direct contrast with impromptu speeches, planned speeches are those that are prepared way ahead of the delivery date. This speech is often given with the aid of a script or a notecard. Usually, planned speeches are given by the President of a country or a company to address his or her subordinates. This may also be given by newscasters and other professionals who need their speeches to be as accurate as possible.

The Subtypes of Speeches

The next types of speeches that this chapter will discuss can fall under either the planned or impromptu speech category. Thus, these can be classified as subtypes. They are more specific than the two main types, and are used for specific occasions.

Informative Speech

As the name implies, an informative speech seeks to spread knowledge, facts or information to the audience. The speaker chooses or is assigned a topic that he or she needs to speak to the audience about using figures, names, dates and events. Examples of informative speech are the speeches given by lecturers or professors to their students.

Demonstrative Speech

You can think of the demonstrative speech as a "How to _____" performance. The speaker is tasked to show the audience how certain objects work, or how they are made. Demonstrative speeches focus on the application of skills to facilitate machines, new experiences and so on. One example of a demonstrative speech is that given by shop assistants who draw in customers by explaining and showing how their new product works.

Persuasive Speech

The speaker delivering a persuasive speech aims to convince their audience that their opinions or ideas are better than that of the opposition. Persuasive speech makes use of both hard facts and flexible opinion in order to win the crowd's favor. Examples of persuasive speech are those used in debates, parliamentary procedures and electoral campaigns.

Special Occasion Speech

This speech is usually used during festivals, celebrations and other occasions. This is based on emotion and conviction. Special occasion speeches are tailored to fit the event and the audience's interests. Toasts, roasts, eulogies and commencement exercises addresses are examples of special occasion speech.

Toast

A toast is a short, witty speech given in honor of a dear friend, an esteemed colleague or a beloved family member. Toasts are usually one to three minutes long, and are often remembered for their humor as well as the memories that the speaker invokes.

Roast

On the other hand, a roast, which is also a short, witty speech, focuses on sarcasm and negative humor, though it is also done in honor of a celebrant. Roasts are more difficult to deliver because of the ill humor required, as well as appropriate sensitivity to the person being spoken of. Still, when a roast is delivered successfully, the whole audience, including the celebrant or person of honor, is left laughing and feeling lighthearted.

Eulogy

Eulogies are speeches given in honor of those who have passed away. The speakers are usually close relatives and friends of the deceased who wish to share memories and thoughts with the rest of the crowd. Eulogies are delivered before the casket is closed and the loved one is finally laid to rest. There is no strict time limit for eulogies because of its sensitive nature.

Chapter 15: I've Got The Dormant Runner Blues

For a runner, there are down days often used for either rest and recovery, or for cross-training. These days are important and since you are a superhuman in training, they are even more important! There are several things about these days that make them good and bad for a runner though. They are bad because you will not be running on these days. That means no light jog around the block just for funsies. You are not running, period, and for some people this can be just heart breaking. Others, especially those who prefer other activities to running may relish their down days.

What is a Rest and Recovery Day?

These can be either an actual rest day where you do nothing but rest or they can be a more active rest day where you do other things that improve your body and inevitably your runs. A recovery day is a more active day meant to give you more flexibility and to lower your chance of injury. Some of the things you should be doing on these days:

Find a good stretching or yoga practice especially one designed for runners. A runner's yoga program should talk about hip opening poses and should include pyramid pose, pigeon pose and several others. These poses will open and stretch those hard worked muscles, so remember, if it bothers you, you need it.

* Side note: in yoga being slightly out of your comfort zone is fine. Being slightly uncomfortable is fine. Having some concern is okay. Being in pain? Not okay at all. If you are feeling actual pain you have pushed yourself to far and need to either back off slightly, or come out of the pose altogether. Don't get hung up on the "new agey" feel of yoga if it's not your thing; there are plenty of practices and instructors who are all about the pose and less about the connection of mind and

body . Keep experimenting until you find the right one.

Learn the fine art of foam rolling. Foam rollers come in many different sizes and textures. A pool noodle can work for lighter muscle work but for those really deep aches and pains you will need the rumble roller. Short and stubby, this guy will be like your side kick and your arch enemy at the same time as those big nubs really grind into your flesh and work out every last kink and knot in your body. You may hate it while you are doing it but you will love how you feel when you are done.

A good soak in the tub is a perfect way to end a rest and recovery day. A soak in Epsom salts is perfect and should be done about twice a week. Another soak is 2 cups of Epsom salts mixed with half of a cup of baking soda. If you happen to have any essential oils around you can add them but they are not necessary. Aim to soak in the tub for at least fifteen minutes and you will feel amazing when you come out.

Cross-training Days

A superhuman cannot just depend on lighting speed or their ability to toss foes like tiny ragdolls. Nope, a good superhuman is a well-rounded human, and that is where the cross-training days come in. On these days you should feel free to do anything that will improve your running, stamina, speed and more. These days should include strength training and other activities like biking or swimming. Strength training is the perfect complement to the runner's training program for a lot of reasons.

Strength training helps to improve the rate of muscle rebuilding. As you run, you damage your muscles, ligaments, joints and bones. Strength training helps the body to rebuild and repair that damage.

Strength training improves stamina and endurance without cardio effort.

It improves your balance as well.

Stronger muscles equal more power, especially when you need it the most.

A good strength training routine will be complementary to your running routine so schedule your sessions on off days. This prevents you from "saving" up energy from one activity so that you can do the other. Like your race training, your strength training should be broken down into three separate stages.

The Starting Position: Building a Solid Base

Whether you are new to strength training or not, this is where you will begin. The focus in this phase is going to be on learning about proper technique and form, for the exercises that you are focusing on. Because you are a superhuman working on the power of the marathon, you will be doing mostly body weight exercises in this phase, especially single leg exercises. Body weight exercises are great because they keep you from exerting too much effort, you are already used to lifting your body weight- you do it every day. Single leg exercises expose imbalances in the body and show you were your weak spots are. For instance, the single leg squat, which is often called a pistol squat can show you that your right leg is both strong and flexible, while your left leg is a wobbly, stiff wreck. That exposure at this stage lets you work on making improvements.

Second Phase: Up We Go!

In the second phase of your strength training days you will be picking up weight. At first, you will use lower weights and higher reps but as the reps get easier and easier the weights should get heavier and heavier. Progress is a continually on going thing in building the perfect body.

Exercises in this phase should continue to challenge things like balance but should also work to improve the strength in your legs, and all other areas of your body.

Third Phase: Dynamic!

Your third phase which should coincide with your biggest push before race day will consist of body weight exercises again, but with a twist. You won't be trying to improve balance or expose weaknesses here! Oh no, you should be well beyond that stage at this point of the game. This phase is about building explosive, dynamic power; the kind that is worthy of a true superhero. You will use the moves that used to impress (and frankly scare you) at the gym, now they are yours to master! Think tuck jump. Think jump squat. Think box jump. Think power. Think explosive power. Think explosive, dynamic power. Gah! It just makes me want to jump over buildings!

Protip: Do not try to jump over buildings.

Chapter 16: Coping With The Unexpected

In any event, there will always be moments that you didn't anticipate. Things can go awry and the only recourse that you have to take is to be prepared for them or deal with them head-on.

Technical Difficulties

Life can be a bitch. You may not want your microphone to malfunction, but it can and it probably will. So, if you ever face this problem, suck it up and put on a calm face. Don't panic. Always be prepared for technical difficulties. Have an extra microphone near you if your current one isn't working. However, if the problem is with the electrical supply, be ready to increase the volume of your voice and let your voice be heard. You can do it. The town criers of ancient times—like grandfathers of modern public speakers—managed to convey their messages just by screaming to be heard in crowds.

If the problem is with your slides or your notes, your rehearsal will come into play and could help you survive even without them. If you have rehearsed enough, you would be able to still speak up because you know the flow of your speech.

Distractions

If you find yourself getting distracted by something in the audience, try to immediately revert your attention back to what you're doing. At the end of the day, you can't really afford ending up blank-faced right there in the middle of the room. Let's say that someone's talking on his phone right in the middle of your speech; look away and focus instead on a face in the audience who's clearly paying attention to you.

Hecklers

Hecklers can get your blood pressure rising. This time around, it's not the fear of speaking that's making you anxious but the desire to literally shut someone up. But chill. Treat hecklers with the professionalism that will paint you in a good light. Politely address their concerns if you can and if they become too much, calmly ask them to wait for the end of the event to discuss things further with you.

Don't lose your cool while you speak because it will taint the whole memory of the event. Public speaking is a communication skill and part of that skill is the ability to talk your way through situations and knowing what to say in specific circumstances.

Handling questions

As you speak or present your message, someone might interrupt you by asking questions. Don't brush them off since that would be very unprofessional. And try doing that if your listener is your boss, hmm?

What you can do is answer the question as directly as possible. You don't want to have your time shaved off by half just to answer questions, leaving the rest of your content unspoken. Moreover, be careful with your behavior in answering them. The way you handle one question could set the tone for the remaining time of your speech. If you respond negatively to an inquiry, this may discourage and turn off your audience and make you look aloof.

Furthermore, you should also remember to address your answer to the whole room so that other people can benefit from your response. To add, ask the inquirer if you have satisfied him or her with your answer.

However, if a person ends up getting persistent with his questions, ask calmly and politely to stop and contact you or get in touch with you after the presentation so you can accommodate him.

Chapter 17: Don't Allow Stage Fright Stop You From Making A Powerful Speech

A Wall Street Journal survey showed that the biggest fear Americans have is public speaking – not fear of death, clowns, heights, flying or driving – but public speaking.

Just think about how hard it is for a shy person to actually talk in front of a group of people – that they would rather wish for death than have to do this.

Stage fright is a real thing – doesn't matter if you have to give a speech, talk in a group discussion or do a presentation. Many people don't have a flair for talking and often stumble through things in the hopes to get them done and over with.

Visionary Elon Musk is well-known for stammering through a presentation, so just think what the average person goes through when they need to speak to the public.

The fear of failure, the fear of people laughing at them, the nervous breakdown and anxiety – it's all associated with public speaking. These thoughts can affect how a person feels about themselves, lowering their self-confidence and self-esteem.

But, with a bit of learning and continuous practice, you can deliver the kind of public speech that captivates and motivates your audience. So, if you need some help to make that happen, there are a few things that can assist you:

Learn About Your Audience

Who are you talking to this time? Will the audience be a group of novices or professionals? Are you talking to a local group or out of town group? Make sure the content you're going to be discussing is relevant to the audience you are giving a speech to.

You want them to stay engaged and interested in what you have to say. Do not make jokes in front of groups that may take offense to them. You don't want to make an awkward situation even worse for your audience and yourself.

Breathe Deep and Give Yourself A Pep Talk

If you have speech anxiety, the best thing you can do is take slow deep breaths. Public speaking coaches teach students that breathing deep can alleviate the stress they feel and calm themselves down.

Shallow, quick breaths only cause even more anxiety especially when you're about to go on stage. So, before you need to go on stage, you need to take a deep breath and calm your nerves.

Remember positive affirmations such as:

Just be yourself

I can do this

You can have fun

This isn't about me; it's about them

Nervousness Is Human Nature

It's only human to be nervous when you're doing something, you're not comfortable with. However, you can ease your fear and anxiety by reaching out to a close confidant or relative.

You can also break the ice with your audience with a clean joke (or imagine the audience in their underwear). The majority of people in the audience do not envy you; they don't want to be giving a speech.

Do A Practice Run and Seek Feedback

A week or two before you need to give your presentation or do the speech, practice them in front of a mirror then in front of family and friends. You can also do it in front of a small group of strangers.

The idea is to see how you can improve your public speaking skills, get familiar with speaking in front of others and look for feedback from these individuals.

What did they see that you could do differently? The key is to deliver a flawless speech when you need to give it.

Be On Point With Your Speech

Your speech should be on topic and precise to maintain the audience's attention. You don't want to forget what you're talking about. Be sure it's captivating so they'll want to continue listening.

Don't use jargon (unnecessary words). Make use of audio-visual tools to engage the audience even more. Have a Q&A session after your speech is over, but have answers prepared for different types of questions.

Chapter 18: Proven Ways To Grab The Audiences' Attention

If you have been waiting for the moment I tell you how to make your speech more than just good, but amazing, then this is that moment. In this chapter, I'm going to tell you how you can grab ahold of the audience verbally and keep them enraptured with your words. It's all about their emotions and how they're interpreting what you're saying, and you can really keep them engaged with a few simple tricks.

#1 Give Them Something to Take Home

Provide something specific for the audience to take home with them. It doesn't matter how inspiring your message is, every audience wants to learn a tangible way they can apply what they've learned to their lives this moment. So don't be afraid to tell them to do something that night, right away, and then tell them how they can fix it tomorrow.

#2 Don't Defer Questions

If someone has a question in the middle of a presentation, that's an amazing thing! Someone is actually listening to what you're saying! Seize that opportunity and address their question, even if it's further along in the presentation. Practice skipping around so you can do this if a question comes up. The best presentation is going to feel like a conversation, even if that conversation is one-sided. So don't ever ignore someone's question.

#3 Ask Questions You Can't Answer

When you ask a question to engage your audience it usually feels forced. Instead, ask a question you know they can't answer and tell them it's okay, you can't answer that question either. Explain why you're not able to answer that question and then talk about what you do know about the topic at hand. Most speakers tell you they have all the answers, but if you tell the audience you don't and you're willing to admit that honestly, then that humanizes you and make the audience pay attention to what you do know.

#4 Fuel Your Mental Engine

Did you know dopamine and epinephrine help regulate your mental alertness? Both of them come from tyrosine which is an amino acid found in protein. Therefore include protein in the meal before you do your speech. Don't wait until the last second because the last thing you're going to want to do is eat before a public speech.

#5 Burn off Some Cortisol

This is dispersed by your adrenal glands when you're feeling stressed or anxious. High levels can limit originality and the capability to process information, and when you're high on cortisol, it's almost unmanageable to react to your audience and read them. The easiest way to burn that off is to exercise. Work out before you go to work, take a walk at lunch, or hit the gym before you go to a speaking engagement.

#6 Make Contingency Plans

I don't think I can mention this enough. Come up with all the 'what ifs' you can and answer them. Such as, what if there's a fire during your speech? What if someone asks a question you can't answer? What if you suddenly lose your voice? All of those are things you should think about and try to come up with what you might do. Odds are none of those things are going to happen, but thinking about what you'll do in that situation and having a plan for it will make you feel more confident while you're on stage. You'll have a clear idea of what you'd do in a 'what if' situation.

#7 Make a Pre-Routine

Instead of having superstitions like a lucky pair of socks or a lucky bracelet, make a routine that allows you to center yourself emotionally. Walk into the room you'll perform in ahead of time to check sight lines. Check the microphones and go through your presentation at the sight before it's time to do the speech.

#8 Set a Backup Goal

What if you're speaking to a charity and your presentation starts to fall flat? In response, people will try too hard or give up. If your goal is to land a contract and you believe you won't succeed, shift to trying to plant the seeds for a future speech down the road. If you see you won't get what you want right away, why can't you make room to try again in the future?

#9 Share an Emotional Story

We all have ones. Everyone has a moment in their life that was really emotional for them, and you don't necessarily have to use yours. Tell a story that will capture the audience and be emotional about it. If you feel sad, show it and tell them how you felt. If you felt angry or hurt, tell them. If you cried, tell them. When you share your true feelings about a story, you create a lasting connection with your audience.

#10 Pause for Ten Seconds

Pause for just three seconds and the audience thinks you lost your place. Five seconds and they believe it's an intentional pause. Ten seconds and the ones who got lost or started texting are now looking up. When you start to speak again, they assume the pause was deliberate and you are a poised speaker. A poor speaker will abhor a vacuum, only self-assured speakers are confident with their silence. Take a long pause to gather your thoughts and the audience gives you speaker bonus points.

#11 Share Something They Don't Know

No one ever says something about the fancy chart you put on the screen, but if you tell them their stomach lining blushes when their face blushes, they won't forget it anytime soon. Find something fun, interesting, and different to share with them and they will immediately start paying attention.

#12 Benefit the Audience

Stop thinking about sales and start thinking about what you can tell the audience that will benefit them. Put your focus on being sure the audience will benefit from what you say and they will automatically listen.

#13 Don't Make Excuses

Don't tell an audience you're not good at something or you didn't have enough time to prepare. They will automatically get angry that you're wasting their time. Just go ahead and do it, and forget about the excuses.

#14 Don't Do Prep Onstage

Do not wait until you're on the stage to check lighting, the mic, the remote, or the presentation. Do all of that before the audience fills in so you look set up and ready to go. If there are people who run those functions, talk to them to see what can be done if something goes wrong. And if something does go wrong, smile and look confident while you or someone else takes care of the problem. Your reaction is the most important part of whether or not something goes wrong.

#15 Don't Overload Slides

Make sure the font size is double the average age of the audience. So the font should be between sixty and eighty in size. If you need to fit more words on, then you haven't tightened the message.

#16 Don't Read Slides

The audience should be able to scan the slide, not have to read the slide. If they do, you'll lose them. And if you read them, you'll most definitely lose them. The slide is the accent point, not the actual point.

#17 Focus on Attention

Instead of telling people to turn off their cell phones and making yourself look like their teacher and not an equal, focus on earning their attention. That's right, earn it. Make the presentation so interesting and entertaining they won't want to look at their phones. It's not their job to listen to you, it's your job to make them want to listen.

#18 Repeat Audience Questions

Unless a microphone is being used, it's unlikely everyone in the audience heard the question another audience member asked. Repeat the question and then answer it so people know what you're talking about. It's courteous and provides you with some time to think of a great way to answer the question.

#19 Repeat Yourself

The audience is going to hear about half of what you say, and then they're going to filter in with their own perspectives. Create a structure that lets you repeat and reinforce your key points. First explain the point, and then give some examples of how it can be applied and at the end the audience has action steps to take home.

#20 Run Short

If you have thirty minutes, then take twenty-five. If you have an hour, take fifty minutes. Always respect the time of your audience and end a little early. As a bonus, you hone your presentation and can shift gears if the presentation takes an unexpected turn. Finish early and ask for questions. Invite them to see you after the presentation. Never run long because all you just told them will most likely be forgotten.

And that's how you make an amazing presentation!

Chapter 19: Communication In Marriage

In marriage, the ability to communicate properly is essential for the relationship to be stable and happy. And the good thing is that this is an art that can be learned.

Communication consists of several elements: there needs to be a person who has something to say and someone who hears the message. In turn, the quality of the message will depend on the clarity to communicate and the willingness and ability of the recipient to listen. The more specific, short, direct and interference-free the channel we use to communicate, the message can be heard more clearly. For example, we should be able to say: "I am upset (or) because yesterday when I asked you if we could plan a vacation, you answered me very beaten and from Malaga."

Likewise, the feedback that the listener gives to the sender is very helpful for the communication to succeed. Feedback is to paraphrase what you heard or think you heard; For example, he can say: "So you are upset (or) because yesterday it seemed to you that I spoke to you beating and reluctantly." If the receiver does not offer that feedback or shared meaning, perhaps the sender can ask the other person to repeat what he thinks he heard.

Communication also interferes with what is known as "communication hindrances." Here are some of the most frequent:

Lack of clarity in the message or language: Remember to be specific and above all bring only one issue at a time. Think about what you want to say and how you will say it. What is the best language and vocabulary you can use with the person with whom you want to communicate? Remember that the purpose of communication is to be understood so that the other can respond to our expressed need.

Emotional noise: This depends on how people are feeling: For example, if a person is feeling little appreciated, that feeling will affect how he transmits or hears what his partner wants to say. Therefore, if the couple responds badly to a simple question, ask with concern, what happens to you? You feel good? Also, try not to try to solve problems or express your opinion when you are in an altered state. Wait for the adrenaline to disappear from your body and when you feel calmer, start the communication again.

The tone of voice and inappropriate accentuation of words: Notice how he says things. It is not the same to speak with a derogatory tone or to shouts than, to begin with, kindness. The tone of voice and the accent help create the right environment for communication. There are those who are intimidated with certain tones of voice.

The negative attitude of the listener: To succeed in communication, the person with whom you want to communicate has to want to communicate. It is preferable to make a session and wait until that person is ready to start the conversation.

The environment around them, the time of day, the noises present: Do you remember how much you thought about where and how you were going to propose marriage? Why stop doing something that was possibly successful? Think, and choose the best time. Experience tells us that the best time to resolve a conflict is not when you are angry. Wait until it has calmed down then choose the place and time.

When we know the communication style of our partner, we can improve our communication and possibly better understand their attitudes.

We also have different ways or styles to communicate, depending on our personality (introvert, extrovert, etc.) or what we have learned through our personal experience.

- We often think that the way we communicate is the best (the lion thinks they are all in the same condition) and we don't realize that other people can have a different way of communicating without necessarily being wrong. For this reason, it is convenient for everyone to examine their communication style and then stop to observe how their partner communicates.

• Ask yourself for example: Am I an introvert or an extrovert? How to know People who enjoy the company of other people and get energized when they have someone to talk to and share their time with are usually outgoing. On the contrary, people to whom being among many people exhausts them and prefers the company of a few or requires many moments of solitude may be introverted. Extroverts like to express what they are thinking and share it with other people while introverts like to first process their thoughts in silence and then express them. Neither way of being is better or worse. Each has its advantages and disadvantages that can be taken into account for the relationship. But knowing each other's style is already a good start.

- When we know the communication style of our partner we can improve our communication and possibly better understand their attitudes. Occasionally, both may have the same communication style (introverted or extroverted). However, usually one will be more or less than the other and therefore have to learn to communicate properly with your partner

Now that you have reflected on your and your partner's communication style, what do you think you can do to be more successful in your communication?

Communication, as well as love, is expressed in many ways. In the case of marriage, these two are very close. Pay attention to how you like your partner to be flattered. Some couples like loving and affirming words; others prefer that you spend time with them. Other couples feel very flattered when you give them a gift or make them their favorite food and others prefer that you offer them a service and help. For some couples, physical contact is very important and flatters them that you take them by the hand or give them a message.

We often think that what we like or rejoice will flatter our partner. However, with time and observation, we realize that this is not such. Communication between couples should improve over time. Couples the more they know each other can be more attentive to each other's needs.

THE IMPORTANCE OF COMMUNICATION IN MARRIAGE

The power of communication in marriage cannot be overemphasized. "We need to talk," is a phrase commonly used by couples, when their relationship has encountered interpersonal bumps and they need to fix things. Through communication, difficult situations are resolved and doubts are cleared. Through the use of proper communication, malice, fighting, high blood pressure, and divorce are avoided; while happiness, harmony, progress, mutual respect are experienced.

- Sticks and stones are hard on bones
- Aimed with angry art,
- Words can sting like anything
- But silence breaks the heart.

The above verse was a creation of Phyllis McGinley for "Ballade of Lost Objects" in 1954. It shows the importance of communication in human relationships. Communication can never be too much in a marriage. This is because every aspect of the home depends largely on the abilities of the couple and their children to communicate effectively with each other. Communication has always been the biggest problem whenever and wherever husband and wife tried to co-exist.

When two people are emotionally committed to each other, communication problems are those bumps in the road which make their journey rough and put the stain on the relationship's machinery which the couple built with love, care, and mutual respect. Bottling up issues often create a rift of dissatisfaction, which ultimately breeds discord and dejection. But constant communication in the home will result in the growth of understanding and affection, an increase of trust and intimacy, as well as relief and reconciliation where there have been emotional thunderstorms.

There are a number of things that couples need to frequently discuss. These include:

- Plans and aspirations. You need to discuss your plans and aspirations and desires for your family and agree on the best way to go about them

- The upbringing of the children. This is the collective responsibility of the husband and wife so it must be discussed and reasonable conclusions reached.

- Finance. This is a crucial issue in every home. It is one of the greatest causes of crises in a home. How the incomes and expenditures must be balanced have to be discussed. In fact, this should be discussed as often as possible because of its importance.

- Offenses. When two people live together it will be impossible not to offend each other once in a while. When this occurs you should be willing to speak up in love instead of sulking, nagging or murmuring about it.

- Your relationship. You should discuss your relationship as often as possible trying to find a way to improve it.

- Every other area of interest concerning your home should be discussed and not neglected.

The communication should take place in such a way that it will be harmonious and friendly. To do so there are rules that must be observed.

Time: In today's hectic life when couples are participants in the rat race for wealth, quality time doesn't come easily. Time has to be created. This should when both of you are relaxed. Yes, it is possible; all it takes is a little prioritizing on your part. When you want to discuss, switch off the television. Take this opportunity and talk to each other on any topic of interest. It could be on how you spent the day, plan for your next vacation, reminiscing on your early dating period, or discussing some bestseller novels.

Patience: encourage the less loquacious partner to speak up and express his or her opinion. Rather than expecting him or her to speak up, explicitly ask for it. Strike up conservation on a general issue, such as the forthcoming election or tax reform and ask for his or her view on it. Adopt a learner's posture and let your spouse know you are listening. This will encourage him or her to communicate more freely and frankly. You can both learn something besides warming up to each other and enjoying equally balanced conservation.

Most problems in marriage arise because a spouse doesn't understand what others want. There are things that you might expect your spouse to understand without mentioning it. At other times he or she might not have heard what you said. Tell him or her, what you want. However, at the same time he or she might act stubborn, don't mind. Discuss with your partner. You stand a better chance of talking it out with your partner rather than sulking in silence.

Learn to express your feeling clearly. But do it politely and lovely. Keep emotion under control. Identify the problematic areas and concentrate on solving them without attacking personalities. Overlook trivialities. Endeavor to involve your children in the discussion especially when the issues concern them. Remember to always pray together. A family that prays together stays together. As you begin to spend time together with your spouse and children communicating with yourselves, you will begin to experience a depth of love yet unknown, unseen, and unfelt in the family before. Don't let inadequate communication break up your home. Keep talking.

DEFINITIVE SOLUTIONS TO IMPROVE MARRIAGE COMMUNICATION

Utilizing good communication skills is essential for a happy and lasting marriage. Fortunately, it is easier if both are interested in improving as a couple.

The first step to healthy communication is to ascertain your wedding expectations. Once you realize that your spouse will not read your mind and change much after the ceremony, it is time to start communicating.

Here are some skills we need to develop to build healthy communication and help marriage:

1. Eliminate all distractions

To start a conversation by paying attention to the other person and really demonstrating the importance of marriage, you need to turn off TVs, cell phones, computers, etc.

Learn to listen. The world itself has the qualities of a good communicator based on his experience of being a good speaker. In fact, a good communicator is one who listens more than he speaks. Listening is more than just keeping your ears away from distractions, it is paying attention to what the other person is saying.

2. Consider each other's feelings.

A good friendship consists in putting ourselves in the other person's shoes. And in a marriage, this is paramount. Day after day we will be getting to know each other better. We come from different families, with different experiences, values , and expectations that make up the person we are. Instead of being disappointed or nervous when your spouse does not understand or promptly respond to your desires, try to understand it yourself: where it comes from, the experiences you have had, or even haven't had.

3. Create a plan for tough issues

In some circumstances, conversations may be more heated. Many times you will need to talk about difficult issues such as infertility, the other's family, money, death, among others, where patience and empathy must be exercised more than ever. Start in a subtle and peaceful way.

When conversations heat up and love tends to hide, the most important thing at these times is to escape a fight. Take a break in the middle of the conversation and return when both are calmer.

4. Find a solution together

We have to be flexible for a marriage to work. There is much to give and receive, that is, both must give in to certain wills for understanding in order to come to an agreement. After a conversation, enter into an agreement that you both feel comfortable with and keep your word. Be loyal and put into practice what you agreed, otherwise new discussions will arise on the same subject.

5. Find time to communicate.

We have a very busy routine in our daily life. Younger couples usually study and work. Many have small children and many other activities. Understanding and patience are indispensable.

It is important that you find at least 15 minutes every day to:

- Look into each other's eyes.
- Talking about it was their day.
- Remember the goals.
- Assess whether or how they were put into practice.

These actions help not let this kind of synergy fade away.

6. Enjoy each other's company

Successful communication within a marriage happens when two people are comfortable in each other's presence. This includes being comfortable being who you are, taking time to relax, enjoying the moment with you, going out to date for a while, keeping the flame of the love that brought you together. After all, we were born to be happy.

Chapter 20: The Grand Finale. Inciting Action In Your Final Minutes

The success of your entire presentation rests on whether or not your audience takes action. If that seems like a lot of pressure, don't worry. I will show you how to incite action. It only takes one story.

You are down to your final minutes of influence. If you have done your job well, your audience is engaged, inspired, and ready to act on the frameworks you provided. Your last responsibility is to take your audience's desire to implement your frameworks into implementation itself. Many speakers miss this opportunity for a number of reasons. The most common mistakes occur when a speaker attempts to cram 55 minutes of training into a five minute recap, spends the last three minutes of their speech talking about themselves, or wastes the last minute making hard sales from the stage. These approaches almost always lose their audiences. They rarely incite action. This is problematic because the success of your presentation rests on whether or not your audience takes action. I know I repeated this. It's important.

A strategic story at the conclusion of your presentation is key to inciting action. It cannot be just any story. It must mirror the exact action you want your audience to take next. If you want your audience to leave motivated to take risks and make positive changes, leave them with a bold and inspiring story. If you want them to leave introspective and self-reflective, your story should match that theme. I will clarify with an example.

There are different meditation conferences and retreats across the globe. Thousands of people gather for these retreats. One of my clients was a well-known meditation trainer in North America. She was the featured speaker at several of the conferences. After her first round of speeches, she contacted me. She felt her closing remarks were not working for her audiences. She offered to hire me to attend the presentation and advise her. I agreed.

She spoke in front of a group of high school teachers. They wanted to master meditation and eventually teach their "at risk" students how to practice. Her speech walked the audience through her life journey. She shared the successes she had with "at risk" youth by using the meditation techniques she taught the audience. They loved her story. She maintained a calm tone throughout the speech and everything worked. As she delivered her closing remarks, I realized why she felt she was losing her audience at the end. Because she was losing her audience at the end. For whatever reason, she closed with a high energy and intense series of commands. "We need to provide our youth with alternatives to drugs! We need to keep our kids mentally healthy! We need to calm the minds of our future leaders!" and so on. The tone of her voice rose with each command. By the end of her speech, she belted orders. This closing was not effective for her. Her tone during the speech was calming and reflective.

More importantly, the exact next action she wanted her audience to take was to create a meditation program to share with their students. The focus of this practice was on calming the mind and showing its power in non-aggressive ways. Her screaming affirmations did not match that tone. It felt more like boot camp, which is basically the opposite of meditation.

We met and I suggested a simple tweak in the final few moments of her talk. I assured her it would be a game changer. She agreed to test my suggestions in her following speech. At the next conference, she concluded her talk by asking the audience to close their eyes. She gently led them through these words and paused briefly for a deep breath between sentences. She began.

"I believe we need to calm our minds so we can control our bodies. Once we have mastered our minds and bodies, we can begin to live our most productive days and lives. We can then influence our friends, family, and community. Our community goes on to make the world a more peaceful and intentional place, all because of our meditation practice. You can have that practice. Our youth can have that practice. Our world can have that practice. And it all starts with implementing the five steps to starting a sustainable meditation practice that I shared this afternoon. Peace be with you as we implement this massive change, together, today."

What happened next was magic. The complete stillness and calm of the audience lasted for a solid minute before the energy erupted into a standing ovation. There was a renewed sense of excitement from the audience. For the next several months, the speaker received calls and emails about the impact her speech had on those in attendance.

As you consider your closing remarks, what do you want your audience to do next, and what story will you tell to incite that action?

Chapter 21: The Heart Of The Matter:

UNDERSTANDING EXTEMPORANEOUS SPEAKING

What is extemporaneous speaking?

Extemporaneous speaking is speaking from the heart. It can

also be defined as the art of speaking without notes that

is, breaking away from the habit of reading speeches to your

audience.

Many people think and define extemporaneous speaking as

impromptu speaking and by that they mean speaking without any

preparation. I differ with that understanding, extemporaneous speaking has to do with all the preparation that a smart and

effective speaker has to do. The only difference is that an

extemporaneous speaker breaks away from the dependence of

the written text and taps into the inspiration of the moment by

building authenticity with his or her audience hence appearing

passionate and believable.

Many people can choose to debate and even refute whether

extemporaneous speaking, what we call speaking from the heart,

is the most effective way of delivery. However, my work in this

book is not to debate with anyone but to seek to penetrate the

souls of men and letting them understand that speaking from the heart is not only the most effective, but the way communication

or presentations was meant to be.

When we first made a decision to set up a public speaking

centre, where people would be trained and coached on how to

effectively and professionally deliver speeches, we knew right

from the beginning that our work was cut out. We knew that

our cutting-edge would be to help people understand, internalize

and deliver speeches from their hearts. It looked difficult to

many prospects when we shared with them our 'philosophy' of

extemporaneous speaking, but with training, motivation, skill

and smart work, many trainees began to realize that it can be done and that it is the most fulfilling method of communication

that one would want to engage his or her audience.

from the Heart

To date, I have used this 'philosophy' and it has worked. I have

had the opportunity to speak extemporaneously to more than

100,000 people, trained and coached more than 1000 people on

Public Speaking

how to deliver speeches extemporaneously and the results are

amazing and fulfilling at the same time.

2 Dan Mugera

Can it be done? "Yes" it can be done.

Get ready, continue reading, imagine you are in a journey of

self discovery and move in a pace which you are comfortable with but also with urgency of desire for self discovery.

As I write and share with you this information and my

experiences in the world of public speaking, I do not come with

an attitude of viewing you as an empty glass which I need to fill

but as a person with potential which I only need to make you

aware off.

What Is The Necessity Of Public Speaking Skills?

Public speaking or communication skills are not optional.

It is often said that the success of your leadership and your

relationship with other people depends to a great extent on your

ability to communicate. John Maxwell reflects on this and says,

"Many of the great thinkers are not leaders, why? Because they

cannot communicate."

The truth is, today, regardless of your professional background

you will always be required from time to time to stand and speak

before an audience. Equipping yourself with the right public

speaking skills before that day will enable you to be effective and

influential. It is common knowledge to note that, the world over;

men and women who were and are able to organize their thoughts

and speak from their hearts have always risen to greatness in

their fields of endeavor.

From Jesus Christ to Jonathan Edwards, Paul of Tarsus to

Patrick Henry, Martin Luther King Jr to Mother Teresa, Julius 3 Nyerere to John Hagh, Buddha to Barrack Obama, Patrice Emery Lumumba to PLO Lumumba. All this men and women knew and some continue to know the value of public speaking. The power of the spoken words has enabled men to persuade with strength, describe with charisma, narrate with passion and argue with facts.

From the world of religion, politics, business, science and technology, sports and entertainment, public speaking skills has produced outstanding ministers, shaped transformational leaders, great teachers, inspiring and creative coaches.

Therefore, the art of public speaking especially speaking from

the heart cannot be taken for granted.

The world is ruled by public speakers.

What Is Public Speaking?

Public speaking is a public utterance of the man or the woman

herself. When you are communicating you are simply expressing

your beliefs, convictions and principles. This forms the sum total

of your thoughts and experiences. Therefore, it is of necessity to

state that for the purpose of our learning, public speaking is not

primarily externals, imitation or conformity to standards at all. It

is the being, thinking and feeling of the person, so that the man

from the Heart

becomes a veritable messenger of the message he is passing to the audience. Without this, there is no help. Why? Because the speaker can simply become a talker or producer of other men's

Public Speaking

goods by accumulating materials from other people or even read a speech which is a product of another person.

4 Dan Mugera

My experience in public speaking has taught me that the speaker is not dependent on other people's thoughts. He learns sometimes through interaction and sometimes through lonely and quiet moments to gather, arrange and cherish his substance from within as he anticipates how to deliver it. It is this joyful

and sometimes painful experience which enables one to form a

rich and beneficial speech bank.

Externals, Imitations and Patterns

While externals have a place in public speaking, it is important

to note that by 'themselves' they are not public speaking. As a

speaker I know the place of grooming, public address system,

proper venue, podium and even gestures. However, these

things by themselves are not public speaking. For example, it

is important to dress smart and appropriately, but sometimes I

have seen speakers who appear smart outwardly but when they

begin to speak you realize they are bankrupt of ideas and lack the

power and the skills to deliver the speech.

Gestures are also important, but you cannot predict the way

you will use a given gesture before an audience. For example you

cannot plan that as you introduce yourself, you will raise your

right hand, then after five minutes you will push your head back

then point your finger forward, and after ten minutes move away

from the podium and go close to the people as with your hands up.

You cannot do that, this is because you will appear too mechanical

and artificial. Though gestures need to be encouraged, they are

natural ways of expressing oneself based on the personality and

5 learned behavior. It cannot therefore be predicted.

It is important that the students of public speaking learn

from experienced speakers and as well as other coaches without

imitating them. We are all different, created with unique

personalities and orientations, and therefore need to strive to be

original and build our own brand of public speaking.

Can you imagine if a person with a choleric temperament

thus extroverted, hot tempered, quick thinking, active, practical,

strong willed tries to communicate like a melancholy, who is

introverted, logical, analytical, private and a factual person?

What will happen? Most definitely, there will be great conflict.

This is because a choleric is trying to be the person he is not. This

is however evident in our every day interactions. For example,

in places of worship we find preachers who try to preach like

fellow preachers while rationalizing it in the spiritual premise

of impartation from the person they are imitating. This happens

even in politics. If you are a public speaker it is instructive to note

that you cannot hide this reality of imitations especially when

speaking among public speaking students. They can oftenly

notice when you are not being yourself in your demonstration of

your skills in public speaking.

Always strive to be original in your speeches and you will earn

from the Heart

your place among respected speakers.

Finally, let us explore the fact of conformity to patterns.

Whereas I take cognizance of the schools of thoughts in public

Public Speaking

speaking as well as organizations which focus on training people

in public speaking my conviction is that public speaking is not

6 restricted to the given patterns.

Dan Mugera

What do I mean when I speak about patterns? These are

features of communication adapted by the organization training

or coaching individuals in the arena of public speaking. In this

sense, there is almost a stereotypical and predictable presentation in all the speakers that submit to the same school of thought or

training. For example, let us consider this illustration of speakers,

Dan and Pauline.

"**My name** is Dan. Today I will speak to you about character. **The**

definition** of character- character is the belief in an absolute system

of right and wrong combined with the will to do what is right

regardless of the personal cost. A story is told ... let me share with you

three points which can help you become a person of character ...".

"**My name** is Pauline. Today I will speak to you about love.

The definition of love-love is the expression of positive feelings of

goodwill and passion from one person to another. **A story is told** ...

let me share with you three points which will help you develop love …".

Do you notice any common pattern about the two speeches

from Dan and Pauline? Yes, indeed there is a systematic routine

and fixed pattern. Public speaking is not a pattern but it is about

creativity and spontaneity. It is a creative art rather than science

that is predictive. Like an artist, the public speaker should be,

think and feel their own speech before and during its delivery. It

requires skillfulness that is weaved with ones unique personality,

experiences and exposure.Lets me share with you my personal

experience that underlies my philosophy of public speaking from

the heart.

7 My spark

Growing in Likoni on the southern part of Kenya's beautiful coastal city of Mombasa where Swahili is the main language. I developed mastery of the language. The flow, punctuation and grammar of the language saturated my life's communications when talking, joking, arguing, narrating, reasoning, learning and playing. As a young boy I went to two nursery schools within the same vicinity, therefore my fluency in the language was further nurtured. I vividly remember some of my teachers, Mwalimu Mwanasiti, Mwalimu Mwanakombo and Mwalimu Rachel.

('Mwalimu' is the Swahili name for teacher).

It is through these esteemed teachers at this formative stage of my educational life that the fire and experience of extemporaneous speaking was ignited in my heart. I deeply cherish and relish with joy the 'story time' in the classes when the teacher would tell us stories and give us the opportunity to narrate stories to the other kids. I would always seize the opportunity to narrate stories to the other kids. This sparked the fire and referred my confidence in public speaking ever since. Particularly, I remember when I took the stage to give a narrative about the hare and the hyena having been narrated to me by my late sister Naomi. I remember how I was able to capture the attention of the kids with gusto

from the Heart

and interest for about twenty minutes.

Evidently, I attained my teenage years with a relative mastery

of public speaking.

Public Speaking

8 Dan Mugera

My fire

Many thanks go to my Sunday school teacher, Patrick, who we

jestingly referred to as 'Madaraka' apparently because he was

born on Madaraka day (1st June, the day Kenya attained its

independence from the colonial rule of the British). He might have

been my 'Madaraka' in helping me to be ware of my voice and gin

my self independence in being a mere 'echo' of others voices. In particular, the unique occasion of when we were preparing to

recite bible verses at the adult church during a special function in

the church that would attract an unusually bigger audience.

Every Sunday school kid was given a scripture to memorise and

get ready to recite it before the congregation on that particular

Sunday. When Mr. Patrick gave me my scripture, Acts 16:31, he

told me that he had chosen me to recite that particular scripture

because he believed that I had a strong voice and I was able to

pronounce the words very well. Wow! Those were unforgettable

words said by my then Sunday school teacher. This was to me

the fuel that was poured on the spark of fire in my heart for public speaking to cause it to be a flame and subsequently a blaze that

culminated into my ongoing impetus to equip others to do the

same. I seek to equally spark the fire of public speaking in your

heart and our key influencers in all sectors of society as was done

to me. The East Africa Centre for Public Speaking and this book

are the fuel resources for you and many that seek to speak from

the heart.

At the age of fifteen I took to the stage for the first time to

deliver the thirty minutes sermon of the day to the Salvation Army

9 Church for close to thirty five minutes. This too became another

significant contribution to my molding as a public speaker.

My flame

Khamis Secondary School remains an equally significant contri–

–butor to my passion for public speaker. At form two I began to

assume leadership roles through different ranks in the Christian

Union. With humility and in retrospect I am persuaded that my

speaking mastery and leadership competencies positioned me

favorably for this privileged recognition. Through this position

I became associated with a non-denominational organization-

Soul Winners Preacher Revival Evangelistic Team(SOWPRET),

ministries international which further helped develop my

speaking skills, relationships and leadership for many years to come. I remain greatly imbued with a sense of deep appreciation

of SOWPRET .The High school and SOWPRET provided me

valuable the opportunities and experience through which I

gained immense confidence in public speaking. This was indeed

a turning point in my life. I established invaluable relationships

that have become my audience as I speak from my heart. My best

ever ready audience from this association was a young beautiful

from the Heart

lady, who would have the privilege of not only listening to my

heart but has since owned my heart. My wife Judith has continued

to fuel the spark to the blaze I have in my heart today for public speaking.

Public Speaking

At the time of completing my 'O'level studies at Khamis

• Secondary School, I had not only become intellectually inspired

but I had passionately stalked the fireinmyheartthroughspeaking

opportunities in the school and other itinerant engagements with

the Church as well as in significant institutions and organizations

across the country

Fanning the flame

Apart from SOWPRET ministries, I took time to be a student

of public speaking, taking time to be nurtured and exposed to

the world of handling speaking in an ethical and professional manner. Immediately after high school I went to be trained

in Christian ministries and I knew from the word go, that the

reason I went for this training was not to become a pastor but to

gain knowledge which would enable me become of influence to

both the religious and non-religious world. How that was going

to happen I did not know then, but one thing I was quite sure

of by then is that the Almighty God had a big plan for me and

it was necessary for me to be sharpened at an early stage in the

areas of leadership, character and speaking skills to enable the

influence to be realized. Those times I should say were not easy

but very painfully chastising. These were times of self-awareness and accelerated personal empowerment. I took great interest in studying history and public speakers who have transformed the world.

We used to wake up at 4.45am and we would go to sleep at 9 p.m in the night. Every minute counted, every time was accounted for and we were expected to be disciplined disciples of time and every chore assigned to us. Life was indeed programmed.

11 Every morning, one student would have the opportunity to speak to the student body and faculty for fifteen minutes.

Fifteen minutes meant fifteen minutes not sixteen minutes.

The content was expected to be well researched and presented enthusiastically. References were supposed to be exact and unassuming. Such was the veracity of the training I got in public speaking. I remember that was the time that I dedicated my life to research and meditation. I developed a thirst for knowledge and how to present it without reading; I delved into the acclaimed Strong Bible concordance for meaning of words in Hebrew, Greek and sometimes Latin. Every time I had the opportunity to do my fifteen minutes speech to the students and faculty, I knew it was a serious affair. I took time to prepare, pray and meditate so much so that by the time I spoke my message, it had become part of me and I believed in every sentence and word which I uttered. This I still practice to date before any speech. Later, I

would get feedbacks from the students and faculty that it was

indeed a good speech.

My approach to public speaking has always been and will

always be very sacred, this is because I have great reverence

for men and women who are created in the image of God who

from the Heart

is sacred. They must therefore be respected and regarded with

importance whenever and wherever we speak any message to

them.

This is what I believe convinced me and pushed me in 2007

Public Speaking

to make a drastic decision not to limit myself to speaking only

- to religious groups but to get into professional speaking and

influence the world with a strong message from my heart. I have

never regretted the decision as thousands of people have benefited

from my speaking engagement in various places.

My major decision in public speaking also came when I joined

the John Maxwell team to undergo a certification program as a

certified speaker, coach and teacher. This has continually built

my skills and business in enabling me to learn from John and his

faculty as well as other team members from all over the world.

The exposure and knowledge I have and continue to receive

cannot be measured or compared to anything.

In this self-discovery journey, I made a distinct recovery of my

passion and purpose in public speaking. I reckon therefore that

every man who took a noble path to bring about noble changes in

their communities and nations were men endowed with speaking

skills, leadership abilities and great discipline. Furthermore,

they sacrificed a lot because they pursued their passion. That

became the force behind their voice as they spoke from their

heart. They certainly did not need to read a written speech or fit

into an archetype of speaking pattern. Right from Jesus Christ to the missionaries who went preaching through the world, Martin Luther King who led the protestant revolution to Martin Luther King Junior who led the civil revolution in America. They mastered the skills of public speaking from the heart.

That was a time of great self-awareness, self-discipline and personal growth for me. It was fanning the spark into a flame of fire in my heart. More was to come. The Blaze!!

13 The Blaze and Trailblazer

In 2008, barely one year into professional speaking, I shared a podium with Professor PLO Lumumba, a leading and respected public figure and speaker then. I was still a young speaker. This meeting had been organized by the motivators club, of which I

was the secretary, at the Royal Court Hotel in Mombasa. The

Chairman of the club graciously appraised me to be the co-

speaker to Professor PLO Lumumba on this auspicious occasion.

I was deeply flattered and yet profoundly honored to share the

stage with such a prominent and acclaimed extemporaneous

public speaker per excellence.

The day was set and preparations made. I was the first to speak

and my topic was "Eradicating a Poverty Mentality". Professor

Lumumba did the keynote speech and we bonded immediately.

After the speeches I escorted him down stairs to board a car to the airport and his parting words to me were "Let's be in touch".

Sure enough, we got in touch soon afterwards when I traveled

to Nairobi for a meeting. Following the discussion, we observed

the gapping need for public speaking institution whereupon

people could be especially charged with skills of extemporaneous

speaking. That became a reality shortly when we established The

from the Heart

East African Centre for Public Speaking.

Since then, my journey in the world of public speaking took a

different turn. What began as a small spark at the nursery school,

become a fire at the High school, became a flame at Church now

Public Speaking

- is ablaze in my heart. It is the heart of the matter. It is the art of public speaking. It is extemporaneous speaking. Moreover, through East Africa Centre for Public Speaking it has now become a trail blazer. I not only delight in being able to enjoy it myself but to also train and coach more people who could be facing all sorts of challenges in mastering this skill.

I am even more enthralled that I am able to package this for you in a book which you can continually refer and share it with others.

By the special grace of God, this blaze has burned through my heart to speak to hundreds of thousands of direct audiences in

learning institutions, churches, corporates organizations, social

gatherings and groups. Moreover, through the strategic television

and radio features I have addressed millions with the message of

extemporaneous speaking.

I will forever be gratefully for the opportunity to impact lives

through public speaking which has brought much fulfillment in

my personal life and to many people and has taught me to know

that the art of public speaking is indeed a vital tool of impact to

the world.

The beauty of it all is that this skill can be learned, developed and mastered for effective public speaking. What is more? This

can be your reality so that you can speak in public from the

privacy of your heart. We will learn more of this in the next

chapter, as we look at how you sharpen your heart with respect

to preparing to do extemporaneous speaking. Meanwhile I invite

you to respond to the following reflection questions in light of

what we have learnt so far.

Chapter 22: Use Visual Aids, Illustrations.

It would be rather unusual in present times to host a scheduled public presentation without a PowerPoint or whiteboard presentation of pictures, graphics, maps, timelines and sundry illustrations. Where you have them, use visual aids well to add colour and vividness to your talk, helping your audience to better understand what you say and to remember for longer periods.

Points to note

Avoid overuse.

Visual aids are easy to abuse. With technology, dozens of aids could be made or generated at short notices, or simply downloaded online in seconds. A speaker may get carried away to present more pictures than are actually needed to highlight the main points of the talk. When overused, the visuals tend to distract, rather than enhance, the quality of your presentation and the understanding of the topic in discourse.

Also, when too many visuals are projected in rapid succession, with no comments by the speaker, they tend to confuse the audience. In your effort to do better in public speaking, therefore, it's advisable you learn how to carefully select the items that would add real value to your talk. Ensure the presentations are cued and ready to go, before you begin the talk, to avoid disappointment. It frequently happens, even in big organisations, for the CEO to call for a visual aid to support ongoing talk, only to discover that the material isn't just ready!

Let the visuals speak.

The aids you show will not speak to the audience if they are not clearly seen or heard. And what is the point of including a visual aid if the audience cannot see it? For instance, it would be entirely futile to play a video on a small laptop in a large hall, when the audience will neither see, nor hear, clearly what you show. Or, you project graphics to the white board but did not leave them long enough to enable all in the audience to even take a look at the materials. You may have to leave the items on, while you make brief explanations to help the audience connect the images to the points being made.

More is gained when members of the audience are given opportunity to comment on the import of any visual aid being used. Aside giving them a chance to be part of the show, audience participation will help you evaluate the progress you're making in sharing your ideas.

Use word pictures.

The masters of public speaking could paint pictures with words of mouth. You can make the points so vivid that the audience would begin to form concrete mental images on the basis of what you say. This happens, especially, when you illustrate the point with familiar objects, the ones in everyday use around the neighbourhood.

Let's assume that you have the privilege of teaching a religious gathering the imperative for God (I'm assuming you believe He exists) to remove wicked people from the earth. You could illustrate the point with a landlord whose property is occupied by irresponsible tenants. Everyone picture the landlord asking for rents, warning against misuse and damage to his building, separating fight among irresponsible tenants, until he decides he's had enough.

What does he do? He issues a quit notice to the bad tenants and subsequently throws them out. It's easy to conjure up a mental picture of the landlord and tenant story, since almost everyone in the audience could related with it.

You can then infer that, God, as landlord of the earth, would feel obliged to remove bad and unrepentant tenants in the fullness of time.

Choose familiar illustrations.

Illustrations are particularly effective if the speaker draws from familiar objects, things that both the speaker and the audience could easily relate to, incidents that are common within the community.

A masterful religious teacher in the Bible times, restricted his illustrations to local bird species, flowers, popular farming activities and common work tools. Look, how great he proved to be in planting his message in the minds of his followers at a time when no other visual aid existed! No wonder some regard Jesus Christ as the greatest public speaker of all time.

Conclusion

We certainly have all been in a keynote display or company address. Typically, the speaker is knowledgeable and adept at the topic, nevertheless talks drones on and on. Skilled public speakers stay clear of this condition by always engaging their listeners.

It goes without stating, but being knowledgeable of your material forwards and backwards is a crucial component — Here are a few guidelines on how to most effectively get ready.

For starters, you should be personable on stage as a way to get your audience intrigued. Through the art of public speaking, a personable lecturer is the best way to get a listener to connect, hence helping to make their speech far more satisfying and educational. Being personable may or may not come naturally to you. If it doesn't come naturally, you still have to find a way to reveal your self as friendly and approachable.

To be personable demands making an attempt to relate together with your audience. In short, it involves simply being present inside the moment. Listeners in some cases will remark that "the public speaker just seemed to be providing a memorized speech and did not appear to be that interested in his subject." It's simply the opposite of a personable public speaker, and you will have to make actions to prevent this reaction.

Start sharing a fascinating narrative that features a true life application to your subject matter. The starting point of the presentation is the opportunity to ease in to the area of interest and set the direction and atmosphere of the time. More essential, its your chance to engage your visitors. An introductory story should offer the framework for your discussion. Effectively, it requires a real life illustration, an instance that every single person in your audience can relate to on some level. This links your subject matter to the listener, and keeps your viewers involved.

Throughout an appearance, a speaker who will poke fun at him or herself, is going to consistently amuse the viewers. As the public speaker, you're going to be quickly placed on a pedestal. You're observed as the guru in the area, and frequently above reproach. Helping to make light of the situation you've already been put within disarms the listener's preconceived notions, and will allow for them to listen to you as a peer. The art of public speaking requires holding your audience's attention at all times. Taking oneself way too seriously will disconnect an interested participant, however making yourself an equal engages the audience.

On top of that, activate your audience by revealing your non-critical weakness. A non-critical weakness is a weakness in oneself that isn't deemed being fatal, harmful, or destructive. Rather, it is more of a personality trait, or maybe a revelation which can be considered endearing. Becoming, a sucker for cookies, disliking to run, humming in the bath to Britney Spears, they are all non-critical weaknesses. By just admitting these to your listeners, you will be confessing that you have faults. And by doing so, you instantaneously achieve their trust. No longer will you be trying to cram questionable realities down their throats. Alternatively, now you've confessed a fault, and thus have put oneself on an even playing field. A revealed non-critical weakness acquires the trust of an audience inside the essential elements of one's public speaking presentation.

True life cases generally strengthen a point, as well as to keep a large group intrigued in your discussion. As the guru on the subject, the majority within the room won't fully grasp the content as effortlessly as you do. Contrasting, your topics with a real life situation to supply assistance, will provide your participants a way to latch on to the ideas. Actual life illustrations give the viewers experiences to relate to the points your are generating, and provide them means to recall your business presentation down the road.

Close your presentation having a personal message about how your topics pertain precisely to the audience. Often times, public speakers make the error of assuming that the concepts they displayed will naturally work themselves into the listener's everyday routine. Don't be so hasty. Presume that it truly is your job to join the themes of your presentation with the listener's daily life. Great presentation skills will be the building block to making your speech more relatable. Put together your discussion to contain experiences and real life illustrations, and make sure to share at least one particular non-critical weakness. Open and close with engaging rhetoric, and your audience will affirm you as a masterful communicator and professional in the art of public speaking.

www.ingramcontent.com/pod-product-compliance
Lightning Source LLC
Chambersburg PA
CBHW072005070526
44583CB00015B/1343